M000288363

WALKING IN MY SHOES...

JACQUELINE RENK

DORRANCE
PUBLISHING CO
EST. 1920
PITTSBURGH, PENNSYLVANIA 15238

Dorrance Publishing Co
585 Alpha Drive
Pittsburgh, PA 15238
Visit our website at *www.dorrancebookstore.com*

ISBN: 978-1-6491-3439-4
eISBN: 978-1-6491-3571-1

I dedicate my life's work to my boys: Matthew, Thomas, and Andrew.
All of you have given me the courage, perseverance,
and grace to move forward
In my life.
I love all of you with all my heart.

Love, Mom

Today is Tuesday, February 11, 2015, Matt and Tommy are twenty years old today. Today I woke up and the only thought that was on my mind was my twins. What could have been? What could have made this day absolutely spectacular? As I got out of my bed, and stepped onto that hardwood floor like I'd done every day, going to the fifth year of Matt's death. I can't believe he's gone. As I approached Tommy's room, of course, he was up with a look of unbelievable accomplishment of where he's been, and where he is today. On the other side, a brief sadness as I grabbed him. I said, "Happy birthday," he grabbed me, and he said, "Thanks, Mom."

Recollecting twenty years ago back at Pennsylvania Hospital was the day of course, I'll never forget. Why I was picked to be a mother of twins? The answer becomes evident at this point in my life, when I look back twenty years. It was actually the day before, February 10, 1995. I went into Dr. Mellen's office to have my twenty-four-week checkup. Dr. Mellen did an internal exam as was the protocol for, a normal pregnancy at twenty-four weeks. After the look on his face, he stepped back and said, "Oh my God," I said, "What's the matter, Doc?" He said, "Well, your cervix is open and the membranes are bulging. You need to go in the emergency room now!" Dave and I looked at each other in bewilderment.

At eighteen weeks I had to stop working because I had Braxton Hicks. I was out of work and on bed rest. I was trying to be in bed as much as I could but the nausea and vomiting lead me praying to the porcelain God! I was getting weary looking into a toilet bowl. Twenty-four hours a day I was vomiting. Dr. Mellen admitted me into the emergency room and started an IV and gave me a magnesium drip. The magnesium was supposed to relax the uterus and keep the pregnancy intact... Dr. Mellen finally came into the room after all the nurses positioned me in Trendelenburg position hoping that if my head was farther than my cervix that actually will close the cervix. "There's a procedure that I could do and it's called a cerclage, but I think it's too late in the pregnancy," Dr. Mellen said. The procedure entails closing up the inner part of the cervix.

Dave was making the calls to alert the family what was happening. Later that Friday night my mom, and my sister came to the hospital. The room was a relatively small room with nurses on top of me constantly taking my blood pressure, giving me more magnesium, and taken every precaution to keep me pregnant. There was another issue going on in my family. Where was my dad? We did not have cell phones back then. My mom was trying to be a mother, but it was hard for her to be nurturing especially at his time.

The center of her life was my dad. She was more concerned where my dad was that night than the matter at hand! She stood by my bedside, giving me ice chips, just the smell of cigarettes on her fingertips made me even more nauseated. I wasn't allowed to drink any liquids just these gross ice chips. I know that my mom was not even there with me. She was physically there, but emotionally and mentally as throughout my whole childhood my mom was never there for me. I was in dire straits and knowing if I was going to survive at this point, let alone my babies surviving. Dave was walking around the ICU bewildered of what's going to happen. Dr. Mellen brought Dave outside of the room, he said, "I have to keep Jackie and I don't know if the twins are going to survive, I need to keep your wife alive." I remember seeing the look on Dave's face. I know he was crying, but he was trying to be strong for me knowing that he could lose his boys, his first two kids. My mother and father-in-law came in and nobody knew how to react. They just didn't know what to say nor what to do to be comforting to me. I just started getting worse and worse.

I don't remember my mom leaving, but I know my sister stayed there for a while. My brother was not present that night. At ten o'clock at night everybody left. Dr. Mellen walked in the room and he said, "I'll be gone for the weekend, but when I come back on Sunday, I want to see you still pregnant." I said, "Okay. I'll do the best I can." Dave and I were expressing the thoughts how are we going to function and move on with the loss of the pregnancy and the loss of these children.

The latter part of the night, the decision was made that we had to deliver. The constant ultrasounds every hour on the hour confirming the position of the boys. Matt was in distress. They called Matt Renk Baby A and Tommy was Renk Baby B. They kept calling Baby A, Baby A, Baby A, he's in distress. They decided to start giving me Surfactin which was a medication which was injected to actually develop the lungs quicker. I recall the injection was so painful that the pain and the burning sensation of the medication still gives me the chills… I was given two injections and the night everything just started going downhill.

I had enough drugs inside me to put a horse down. I recall one of the nurses came in she said, "Mrs. Renk, we need to go into the OR." I said, "What are we doing?" "We got to deliver them now." I said, "I'm not ready. I'm not ready to deliver these babies now." "You're getting progressively ill and we have to take the babies now." I was wheeled into the OR. There were fourteen people in this cold operating room around me. I said, "Well, this is it. I'm going to have them." The confusion, and bewilderment of what's going to happen. My babies are going to be born and I'm not going to see them. The angst of the possibility that my boys could be stillborn. Everything that I hoped for was just going up in flames.

I remember Dave came into the OR, and he was white as a ghost, with his eyes really swollen and standing by me. The nurses were telling me they're going to give me an epidural to deliver Renk Baby A. They're telling me to push and I delivered Matt and he was whisked away from me. I kept calling out and screaming, "I want to see my baby. I want to see my baby." They said, "You can't," I was really getting robbed at the best joy in the world of holding my baby or seeing my baby right after he was born. Matt was brought down to the NICU, which is the neonatal intensive care unit.

Matt was in serious distress. "We're going to bring you back to your room because Baby B was okay right now, and we're going to try to keep you pregnant. We're going to keep you with the one still inside of you." And I was lying there and at this point, it was 3:17 in the morning. The feeling of inconsolable emotional pain torn me into disarray. All I remember is the pain in my chest and tightening in heart. I felt really weak and oxygen face mask was placed on my face. "You're in congestive heart failure, Mrs. Renk. We have to give you some oxygen because your heart is starting to fail on us," Baby B was developing a 105 fever, We have to deliver him right now." This was ten o'clock in the morning and I was in such excruciating pain and I could not breathe, I could not take a deep breath. I still had the persistence and my friskiness about me, I was still yelling at the doctors at some point. I said, "We're not going to do a C section. We're going to deliver him. Give me the Pitocin right now because you're not cutting my stomach open." I kept worrying I got to deliver him because I have to have my twins have the same exact birthday.

I did not want to go through a C section when it wasn't necessary when the babies were so little. "You don't understand. This is an emergency. We've got to get him out right now." I said, "Well, okay. Let's do the Pitocin and get him out now." I was then brought back into the OR, we're back again and this wasn't even a twenty-four-hour period. All of this anxiety, stress, and medical complications that were just going so far south.... The medical team were trying to push for me because I couldn't breathe. Renk Baby B finally came out and when I think about it now, I never heard him cry when he was delivered ... I remember taking a little glimpse at Matt when they whisked him away.

I was back into the recovery room lying here all by myself and nobody came by the recovery room. I'll never forget one of the doctors walking around with two plastic bags with two placentas walking past me. "We're going to take this to the lab."

"What happened!" I just kept saying when could I see them? There was no answer. February 11, 1995 at 11:58 Tommy was born. I was in the recovery room for probably eight hours. It felt like a day or so. I felt the loneliness of sitting there backtracked of the loneliness of being in ICU, and those same feeling came back so surreal these lonely different excerpts of my life just kept coming back to me.

I had the boys at twenty-nine years old. Today, I'm fifty-five. I'm never going to see those babies because I know they're not going to survive. So eventually, they brought me back from the recovery room; I was transferred from recovery to critical ICU. I'm in a room that was the size of a closet.

The boys were in the NICU. Dave's brother, Michael, came into the room with two long stem red roses. He walked over to me and gave me the biggest hug. He said, "Jackie, you are a very, very special person." I'll just never forget that. The look on his face: He was afraid, but he had a glow about him that really made me feel wonderful. My mom and dad came in together. I couldn't even breathe and I was angry all of this family drama going on at a crucial time in my life.... I couldn't even get the words out how angry I was at my dad.

Nobody knew where he was. He was out somewhere.

I did see him the day before when Dr. Mellen admitted me. My mom and dad were talking to Dr. Mellen I guess he didn't think I was going to have the twins. I just wanted my mom and dad to be out of the room because I was just feeling awful. Dave's parents came into the room and they just were ... no words. They didn't know what to say to me either.

I'm in the room and Dave was pacing back and forth. I just kept asking How are the boys? There was ... nothing. I was getting no information of what was going on.....

"You may be able to see the boys tomorrow," Dave expressed reluctantly.

The cardiologist and the pulmonologist entered together, accessing my heart and lungs. I had to keep breathing into this tube. Putting the tight compression stockings on me because I was getting blood clots. The nurses kept saying, "She's getting worse, she's going to have to stay in ICU." "I have to see my boys." "You're not ready to see those boys and they're not ready to see you." The next morning, Dave came in, "I saw the boys," I said, "Well, you didn't see them with me," "You can't move out of this room yet." He said, "We have to make a decision," I said, "About what?" He said, "We have to get them baptized because their prognosis is poor. The boys will not make the next seventy-two hours." At the time we were religious, I should say, if you want to call it that. We followed the Catholic religion. The best idea was to baptize the boys. We had to wait until the next day to baptize the boys. I said, "Well, I have to be there!" I was just lying there in this tiny room unable breathe or see my boys.

Later that day, Tommy coded and CPR was administered for several minutes.... He came back to life! (He gets his feistiness from his mother).

The nurses came into my room with a wheel chair, and told me that the boys will be christened today. Dave gathered the grandparents to come to the christening in the NICU. The La Leche nurses kept coming in and pounding on my breasts, to start the process of breast-feeding. I was just a pincushion; I couldn't even move and they were trying to produce this milk for these premature babies. Matt weighed in at a whopping 1 pound 14 ounces and Tommy weighed in at 1 pound 15 ounces at 12 1/2 inches in length. As the nurses started to help me into the wheel chair, Dave said, "I will warn you that it's not a pretty sight what you're going to see. It's not pretty at all and we are fearful for you—because you can't breathe."

As we approached the elevator, the tension grew in my mind of the unknown of what I am going to see. The nurses were trying to get the oxygen tank secure to the wheelchair, and the mask on my face. Now, I really feel helpless...

As we approached the NICU, my head grew dizzy as we entered the secured double doors. As we entered, the nurse was trying to put a gown on me and made me wash my hands. The loud noises of monitors, lights flashing and beeping were that of a circus. I almost felt like I was at a carnival of all these rides that were happening at the same time. It was so loud! I was wheeled all the way to the back. There were many stages to this unit. There were babies in an isolette that didn't need oxygen. I was wheeled all the way in the back to center and there were two babies lying on these open tables. One was labeled, Renk Baby A and Renk Baby B. As we grew closer to the tables, I just burst out crying, I yelled, "You've got to be kidding me!" I couldn't get out of the chair, because of the oxygen. I asked the nurse if I could touch the boys, as if though I was at a petting zoo. The two nurses said to Dave, "Dave, let's get her out of the chair and let her get up to where she needs to be."

The babies were covered in Saran wrap with a bilirubin blanket, bilirubin light, IVs, and ventilators. Matt had a central line in the center of his head. The chief of Neonatology approached Dave and I, "Once you both are done visiting with the babies, we're going to have to go into the conference room and discuss the boys' prognosis."

Next entering the NICU, was a priest with our parents. The priest was uttering all these prayers, which seemed to go on forever. The priest said, "I need to give them their last rites because of their medical condition."

At that point, I was numb and had no feeling inside me at all, mentally, physically, emotionally, and spiritually I was a wet rag. I couldn't even speak at this point, the unknown future that going through my mind. How could they let me see these kids if they're going to die? Why did you allow me to bond with them? Why did you want me to see them and why do I have to go through this torture of seeing these tiny babies and they're not going to survive? The baptism was over and Dave and I were brought into another room with the neonatologist and gave us the rundown of exactly what happened. The neonatologist said, Matt had a Grade 3 ventricular brain bleed, which, if he does survive, he will have cerebral palsy and never walk or speak. He went on and on with a litany of conditions that the babies would endure if they both survive!

Tommy had a heart murmur. Their vision was a Grade 3 which would lead to blindness, extreme learning disabilities, let alone surviving the vaginal birth. The brain bleed, which Matt developed in the birthing process, was a result from his head not fully developing and softness of skull. The boys actually looked like E.T. Their small bodies measured in length of the size of my forearm, and they both had fur on them. They certainty did not look like babies. I never thought newborns took on recognizable characteristics. As the neonatology team assessed them, we were given what could happen? The only thing that I could do right now was to keep pumping. There was still that window of the seventy-two hours from birth if they're going to survive. I was brought out of ICU and brought into a regular room the next day. My breathing started to improve. Then taken off the oxygen, but still the cardiologist and the pulmonologist were with me constantly breathing into this tube with heavy doses of Lasix. My body was getting swollen from all the medications.

I was approaching day five, of this life altering hospital stay. I remember a lot of my family members came to visit. My Uncle Danny was a very spiritual man I always counted on him for his spiritual intuition.

As he walked in the room, he gave me a big hug and said, "Jackie, those boys are going to be fine. I know they're going to be fine. The Lord is with them and they are going to be fine." I so wanted to believe, but I knew it was Uncle Danny talking. I had to believe him because Uncle Danny was always right. My aunt accompanied my uncle, she has always been very emotionally supportive for me as well. She always filled the void of my mother. My aunt Janice was my mom's sister, she was the one that took care of me most of my life. I applaud her for all she has done for me and she is the reason why I'm here today! I remember seeing the rest of my immediate family members. As the rest of the family entered the room, no one had any words to be spoken. Nobody could see the boys.

The seventy-two hours have passed.

Their chances of survival were getting better. My twins survived at twenty-four weeks!! The emotions could no more than bittersweet situation.

I wanted to get the hell out of the hospital. What am I going home to without my children?

Matthew Robert Renk and Thomas David Renk were both going to be in the hospital for at least the next three months, if they survive. During my short pregnancy of twenty-four weeks, I scanned many baby books to look for the right names for our twin boys. The name Matthew was the first name I came across, which meant a gift from God and that surely was so fitting. Thomas was described as such, bright, cheerful, blond hair, blue eyes with an inquisitive personality. Those names fit their personalities perfectly.

I have my boys, Matthew and Thomas, but they're not coming home with me. I went back to the NICU before I was discharged to say goodbye to them. How are we going to get through this? I remember saying goodbye to them with the feeling of my hands are tied and there's nothing I can do. The feeling of loss and mourning the pregnancy. I was headed into a deep depression and started feeling helpless. All of these unanswered questions? Why couldn't I carry these babies? What was wrong with me? Why is something that made me so happy has now been ripped away from me? In the interim as I was in the hospital, one of my good friends that I met she just had her twins.

Maria was a girlfriend that I met through my twins' organization. The Camden County Mother of Multiples was an organization for multiples, which I joined when I was pregnant. My aunt was telling me about this organization. I went to a meeting around Christmas time, while I was pregnant. Maria and I bonded from the minute we introduced ourselves. We both learned we had the same obstetrician, pediatrician, and we of course would be delivering at Pennsylvania hospital. ...

When Dr. Mellen came back that Sunday night, I remember him coming to my room with his ski outfit on. He said "Didn't I tell you that you still needed to be pregnant on Sunday?" I guess he needed to make light of the situation. He also said, "Well, somebody was asking for you," I said, "Who?" he said, "Maria. She just had her twins." He said, "I don't want you to see her. You have so much going on right now."

She called me later that evening while I was still in the hospital. I just had nothing to say, and she, of course, she didn't know what to say either.

After ten days in the hospital, it was time to go home.

As we left the hospital empty-handed, the emotions were surreal. As I stood standing alone in front of the hospital, waiting for Dave to get the car, I saw all the happy parents leaving the hospital with their babies. I stood at the curb on Spruce Street, watching the cars flying by, and thought that if a car hit me, I would never feel this pain again.

As we drove home, we both had no words to share. We had to stop at Delcrest medical to pick up my breast pump. We had to get the breast pump right away to start pumping breast milk. This was going to be my new twenty-four-hour-a-day job!

As I open up the door, and I walk into the house, and I saw all of these baby items and I review the nursery, which had a Beatrix Potter theme. I was reminiscing on the preparation of the room. I would just walk in the room and say I can't wait; I can't wait!

The cribs were up. Everything was ready, but there were no babies to occupy the nest, which we prepared for them. I collapsed to my knees and just cried. This is just not fair. I came home with nothing. All of that and I have nothing. I just don't have my babies.

I had to pump every three hours. I had to produce this milk that had to be put in the freezer to eventually bring to the hospital the next day. I lived on this breast pump. I was literally pumping every three hours. I was starting to feel like a cow, which had to milked every three hours. Every morning I'd call the hospital at nine o'clock after the doctors would do their rounds.... The same questions I asked each day, "How are the boys doing today? How did they sleep last night?" The nurses would reply, "Oh the boys gained a half an ounce." The boys were gaining weight as the days were progressing. The breast-feeding was helping the boys thrive. I was trying to get adjusted to my new life, my new life of taking care of my twins that were in the hospital.

Pennsylvania Hospital was their best for neonatology. My daily routine would be waking up, ...calling the hospital at nine o'clock in the morning, listen to the rounds, and venture on to get dressed. I would either take the high-speed line to the hospital if I was meeting Dave there that night.... We only had one car at that time. Dave would come back from work and then drive to the hospital. I did have a neighbor across the street, Patty, who would drive me. As the months progressed, I asked one of the nurses, "Can my sister see the boys?"

She said, "Not yet, not yet." Nobody was allowed to see them but the grandparents. My mom never came back to the hospital after the baptism. I knew my mom and dad were having problems, but at that point I didn't really care because I didn't have the energy to care. I had major issues going on right now. I'd go to the hospital each day and sit there for eight hours a day in the rocking chair waiting for the boys to grow. The noises of the unit became a custom to me ears.... Still as I approached the boys in their isolate, I thought to myself what will I endure today at the hospital. I would sit there in the NICU pretty much all day or go back in the Pumping room. I got to do my job, I needed to take a mega amount of brewer's yeast and vitamins to produce breast milk for my twins. By the time Dave got to the hospital I was emotionally spent. I couldn't even, get the words out what happened each day.... It seemed as though the boys would progress two feet and go back five feet each day. I said, "When can I hold the babies?" "How can I get some bonding with my children if I can't even touch them?" The nurse said, "We have to wait till they are at least three pounds in order for you to hold them."

As the weeks went on, one of the nurses said, "We do have something that we can try so you can bond with them. It's called kangaroo care." What this is basically I could bring the babies to my chest, but they couldn't breast feed because they didn't have the capacity and they're on the ventilator.

The boys gained three pounds!

They were putting the ounces on and gaining the weight. The weight was a roller coaster ride. We would move forward and then we move back. I finally got to do the kangaroo care. At least I can do something. The breast milk was placed in the NG tube (nasogastric tube) into the nose and past to the stomach. That was quite fascinating, I sat in the rocking chair and the entourage of nurses saying that it's going to take us a couple minutes to get them off the table onto you. Matt wasn't ready yet. He was just much sicker. I was allowed to hold Tommy. This was a joyous occasion for me to actually feel at least one of my sons. Tom was so tiny and I just felt his little butt in the palm of my hand. "Oh, this is great," this was only a matter of maybe ten to fifteen minutes. I wasn't allowed to hold him too long. The nurses knew I needed something. We're going on almost two months now and it was brutal.

My grandmother was still alive at the time and she would bring over her ravioli. God was she an awesome cook! She taught me how to cook at eight years old. She lived in apartment at my Aunt house. She would have me sleep over when I was a young girl, we watch Johnny Carson, but I was fast asleep before she got out of the bathroom with her shower cap on. she brought food over constantly. I needed to eat a double amount of calories because I was nonstop pumping. My Nannie was the best.

The physical therapist would try to manipulate the boys, so their bodies wouldn't get too stiff lying in their isolette all day. Their care had to monitor at certain points of the day because they would get too stressed out. Blood work in the morning, therapies in afternoon. There were periods of rest between manipulations. The boys knew when I was coming to see them.

As I would walk into the room, they heard my voice and their oxygen saturation would go up. It would be at ninety-nine the whole time. When I would leave the oxygen saturation went down.

The days were, of course, brutal and long. I did this exhausting routine for 110 days. The breast-feeding was really taking a toll on me. It was an absolute walking zombie… I was losing sleep because that's all I was doing, no relaxation in sight for me.

Three and a half months of pumping.

My cousin, Donna, got married that April. I was supposed to be a bridesmaid, and I remember I had to alter the dress because I'd lost weight at that point. I was supposed to be pregnant for the wedding. We still called the hospital every three hours during the wedding to see how the boys were doing. We felt guilty that day because we didn't go to the hospital, but the nurse reassured us, "You both need to just be out of the hospital for one day an and enjoy the wedding."

We thought it was easy for her to say. We tried to have a good time at the wedding. I had to pump at the wedding; boy was that entertaining for all the bridesmaids! I had to pump and dump at the wedding. I had to try to make some normalcy out of the wedding. I remember Dave and I were saying, "Oh, let's go to the hospital and see the boys."

I said, "No, no, no, we can't go to the hospital now." We were so anxious to see them.

We could see a little bit of difference, but I was there every day all day long. I didn't really see much of a difference.

The NICU team were giving them a plethora of medications for their complicated medical conditions... they both had chronic lung disease which would carry them throughout their lives.

Both boys had a Grade 3 retinopathy. The retina would start to deteriorate from the oxygen and being born so early.... Their hearts were great. The lungs were described as wet tissue paper. Matt had an MRI every two weeks to see if he had any residual effects from the brain bleed. The weekly MRIs indicated no change.

Speech pathology came in NICU a few times a week. Matt had the feeding issues with suck, swallow, and breathing all at the same time. The therapist would bring him to the rocking chair and manipulate his cheeks several times to get his facial muscles moving. This was fascinating for me to watch. Thomas seemed to be gaining the weight. Tommy was always progressing a little quicker than Matt. Matt had the issues with his brain; his lungs were a lot worse. He had double chest tubes. Tommy had the one chest tube. After six weeks the chest tubes were taken out. I felt we were subtracting medical equipement.

We were approaching the end of April; we still had at least a month to go before the boys could possibly be discharged. We were starting to see light at the end of the tunnel.

At the end of April, we're starting to do the planning for discharge. How am I going to handle this at home? The final meeting with the NICU team was in position for the discharge. Their chief concern was how were we going to handle these fragile, medically compromised twin boys? The plan was to have nursing care through the night, and a nurse for a few hours during the day.

Tommy was ready to come home, but Matt's not, there goes the bitter-sweet again. I'm so excited that Tommy's going to be able to come home, but in the interim Matt's not ready yet because Matt wasn't sucking, swallowing and breathing on his own. We got to the point that a month before they were going to be discharged, they were off the ventilators. There were a couple incidences through the night that they put them on the CPAP machine. This forced breathing machine that helps with incidences of apnea.

Pennsylvania Hospital was the best neonatology department in the country. We're starting to think about the plan for the boys to eventually come home.

I had enough of the breast feeding. I'm going on three months of pumping. I talked to one of the neonatologists, I said, "I can't do this anymore."

Dave really wanted me to continue breastfeeding and I said, "I physically can't do it anymore.". The formula we chose was for preemies (boy, do I dislike that term). I was making a great decision for myself; by no means was this a selfish decision. I was taking on so many variables at his point.

It was two weeks before Tommy was ready to come home. The whole house had to be cleaned and sterilized. Four oxygen tanks were delivered to the house. Two oxygen tanks in the family room and two oxygen tanks in the nursery, one for each boy, heart-rate monitors, and pulse oximeters. I was setting up the house for a mini-hospital.

Dave was working at Pine Valley Golf Club as a second assistant. How I was going to do this? I had a baby at home and one still in the hospital? Okay. How much more gravy can you put on my mashed potatoes before I start drowning? Metaphorically speaking....

I started feeling I was getting a little bit of energy back. I was cleaning my house, getting everything ready; we had two swings, two little bassinets and two cribs, but the two were not going to be filled. After 110 days in the hospital, Tommy was ready to be discharged. Tommy weighed in at five pounds and five ounces the day he came home—This was happy I wanted to bring two car seats, but I couldn't bring two car seats, bringing the one car seat and I said well, how do I do this? How do I leave one here and bring the other one home? I had to take that day and run with it. My God, oh my God I'm actually putting him in a car seat. We had to put all these blankets underneath him because he was tiny. After putting the nasal cannula on his nose, and his heart monitor in place, we were ready to go. As I turned around, Matt was still lying in the NICU.

I know it was just going to be a matter of time. The only reason Matt was still in the hospital is that he couldn't suck and swallow and breathe at the same time. The speech therapist had to work with Matt a little longer. As I walked over to Matt, I said, "I'll be back tomorrow morning." How am I going to do with two? As we arrived home, I took Tommy Out of the car seat, and held him in our own home. This was a moment I longed for the past three months! I spend days with the respiratory therapist on how the oxygen was going to work in the house.

My house was quarantined. Nobody was allowed in to reduce the rate of infection. That first night was nerve-wracking because if there was an artifact or monitor not picking up, the alarm would go off. I said, "Holy Toledo" we are never going to sleep.

I think I slept on the couch that night. I was too nervous to sleep.

A month before the boys were coming home, the doctors wanted Dave and I to stay in a secluded room at Pennsylvania Hospital with the monitors and oxygen as a trial run. I thought that was pretty cool the way the hospital set up this scenario. The team didn't want the nurses to come in. We called them if we needed them. The nurses only came in to draw the medications .... They were compassionate and supportive.

Then was the countdown till Matt was coming home. I went back and forth to the hospital that week. I sat by myself with Matt all day, while Dave was home with Tommy.

I had to ask the million-dollar question: "What day is Matt coming home?"

Matt's nurse Madeline, said, "He will be discharged on Saturday!"

"Are you kidding me?" I screamed. "We have to get him the hell out of here." She agreed he needed to be with his twin brother.

On May 26 Matt came home. It was actually a whole week right after Tommy. This was one of the best days of my life, such a joyous day. They're coming home after three and a half months in the hospital. It's not going to be a normal homecoming. Nothing has been normal up to this point. I knew I was going to be up all night. I haven't slept in months anyway. The cards that were dealt to us, we dealt those cards, and now time to celebrate with the four of us.

The day of the homecoming celebration we brought Tommy with us. The nurses were so excited to see Tommy. You got so big! You got so big! He gained five ounces, in just one week. He gained a lot of weight being home because we were told, there's a point in the hospital that they stop thriving. They got to be in a different environment and that's when they start growing. As the attending physician stated, "We are putting a lot on your lap, but we have all the supports in place for you." We had a nurse from 11:00 p.m. to 7:00 a.m., and then a nurse from 10:00 a.m. to 2:00 p.m. in the afternoon. In order for me to take care of them all day long I had to have some sort of energy to go… full throttle with two babies.

The day both boys came home, my neighbor next door came running over. "Oh my God, let me see the twins," I gave her a little glimpse of them just because… two babies, two portable oxygen tanks, and two monitors.

How was I going to handle all this?

Nobody was allowed in the house. We hoped for a grand celebration, but we needed time to adjust to our mini-hospital at home.

We knew our lives were going to be life alternating. First, we have twins. Secondly, these dynamic duos are medically compromised.

I had to arrange follow up appointments around nursing care. We traveled with two monitors, two portable oxygen tanks, and two car seats. Those trips to the doctors were, of course, challenging and doing the full exam on them getting blood work to ensure their values were good.

Three weeks after Matt was home, I had to take him back to the Pennsylvania Hospital for an MRI to see if the brain bleed was resolved. We knew at birth with that type of brain bleed, he was going to have residual damage.

He did have many MRIs while he was in the hospital; results revealed the bleed was resolved. A few days after the follow up MRI, I got a phone call from one of the attending physicians. At the time my sister was at my house helping me out. She was a big help when she would come over. Thank God she was there that day!

The physician said, "I want to let you know that we viewed Matt's MRI. Matt was diagnosed with cerebral palsy, and the likelihood for him to walk or speak was very slim."

I felt lightheaded and felt out sorts from the news I just heard. I don't remember what happened after that because I passed out. After I regained consciousness, my sister was talking to me and I told her what happened. We were both hysterically crying.

My sister said, "What does she know? Matt is going to be fine." I don't know what's happening? After the last MRI, the brain bleed was resolved. I think it was just the magnitude of stress that I was going through of physically taking care of the boys and even though I had some nursing care, but it wasn't the same. The nurses were doing what they had to do. I didn't have my mother to help me out and take care of me let alone help me take care of my sons. She was an absentee mom. I was upset and resentful of the fact that my mother never called me once to see how the boys were doing, and if she could help. I guess I thought after this tragic situation, just maybe she would come around. That is what a normal grandmother looks forward to taking care of their grandchildren. For God's sake, what was I thinking? She never took care of me. I had to do it on my own and it was disheartening.

Several weeks later my mom stopped by the house. She needed to vent her issues with my father. She wanted me to hate my dad. I didn't have time for this drama. What she did ask me on the times she did come to the house. "What time is lunch?" I couldn't take care of my mother at this point. I needed to take care of my children and that was the only focus of my life, to the best ability.

I wasn't going out and getting my hair done or going out on dates with Dave. Our job was taking care of these kids day in and day. We were happy that our twins were alive. My mom didn't really understand, and that's where my sister would step in because she knew that my mom wouldn't be there for us.

My sister came to my house every Saturday morning and brought bagels from our favorite bagels shop. She had her own son to care for who was a year old at the time. Dave was working seven days a week. I did look forward to Saturday, to have some sister bonding and have someone to hang out with me on the porch with the boys. I needed another set of hands. At this point it was July, the boys were still on oxygen and monitors. Joanne said empathetically, "I don't know how you do this every day?" When you're chosen to be that special person, you take the challenges with pride.

The hospital called me later that afternoon." It's time to take the oxygen out of the house. The boys have no incidences of apnea." I think I did a cartwheel in my backyard. I called Dave at work with the exciting news.

"The boys are off the oxygen!"

He replied, "What? I'll get home as soon as I can!" Our milestones were quite different than the average parents of twins. As fast as I could,

I took the nasal cannula out of the boys' noses and throw them in the trash! I put the boys in the stroller and walked them around the block, grinning from ear to ear.

"All right. Everything's looking good. There's no oxygen." Dave called our families to come over to share this triumphant moment! Let me go back into the nighttime nursing. Sometimes we did not get the same nurses. The one night I was sleeping and I got up in the middle of the night. The situation was unsettling when a stranger was sleeping in your house. I woke up to go to the bathroom … and the door was shut in the twins' bedroom. I tried to open the door and the door was locked.

I went back to our room, and I said, "Dave, the boys' door is locked." I'm going in there. I knock on the door, told the nurse to "open the door!" and the nurse … she was laying on the floor sleeping and had the boys off the monitors. The next day I called the homecare nursing and told the manager what happened the night before, and she was fired that day.

We have no monitors and the boys are thriving. That physical therapist would come three times a week for therapy with Matt. She would evaluate Tommy every two weeks to see if there were any changes in his development. Tommy did not need the physical therapy.

When Matt came home from the hospital, he would have the shakes. He would be shaking and feel out of sorts, but that was contributed to the prematurity and medications he was on. The sucking, swallowing, breathing, and his low muscle tone in his face. His tongue would stick out a lot because of all those muscles were still immature. The Pediatric Physical therapist would work with him on all of those modalities. Most of her strength training had to do with the brain bleed, the residual effects of the brain bleed attributed to his gross motor skills. She worked on his legs constantly and she made some amazing advancements in Matt's therapy.

Her dedication to his development really shined through. The physical therapy continued for months. At two we reevaluated Matt for speech therapy. Matt was only making sounds, NO WORDS. We found a remarkable therapist in the area. She taught him sign language. The progression of how communication works boggles my mind. The speech therapist would give him all these different signs and we practiced with him at home. We were busy with Speech twice a week and physical therapy three times a week!

We were busy all summer with therapy, we stayed in the house, taking care of our special little miracles. The latter part of August we started planning the christening. We lived in a small house, my mother and father-in-law decided that we could have it at their house. This was a grand event planned by yours truly. We invited well over 200 people to the christening party. We are planning this party (Jackie Style) in a big way. The formal christening mass was held at St. Peter's Church in Merchantville. The party afterwards was day not to be forgotten by all. Dave had a friend who had been member of the Philadelphia Mummers. The Philadelphia mummer's parade has been a Philadelphia tradition, which takes place on New Year's Day, and has been going on for decades. The bands march down Broad Street with all their fancy costumes to celebrate the New Year. As the guests arrived at the house, the Mummers came marching up the street to my In-laws house to celebrate this grand event!

All the attendees at his grand soiree, were outside in the street dancing and mimicking the "Mummer's Strut." It was fantastic to see everyone enjoying the day and celebrating Matthew and Thomas's lives. It was awesome and nobody declined to his or her invitation. My mother-in-Law was concerned, "Where are we going to fit all those people?" "We don't really care. We're doing it."

September was the christening. We had the boys christened as any good Catholic girl would practice. As we roll into October months, speech therapy increased to three times a week, and physical therapy to two times a week. Matt was still not talking, just making some signs.

As Halloween approached us (one of our favorite holidays for Dave and I)—Dave was working at Pine Valley Golf Club at the time—I had this wonderful idea of dressing them as a "DUO," which clearly they were the dynamic duo. I picked the costumes up from the Disney store which were Pooh and Tigger. God, did they look adorable! Tommy was Pooh, because of his plump stature. Matt was Tigger, lean and fierce.

I said to the boys," Here we go. We are going to see Dad!" I put them in their costumes, buckling them in their car seats, and off we went to Pine Valley. I said to myself, Dave is going to freak out when he sees them! We arrive at Pine Valley, the security guard had keen admiration for twins. He's heard about the boys since day one. The guard escorted the boys out of the minivan, and we headed to the office.

Ronnie, the secretary screamed with an abundance of excitement, "Oh my God! Matt and Tommy are here!" The entire grounds crew were paged on the radios to come to the office. Everyone was elated to see the boys especially with their costumes on. Dave was proud of his boys, and quite surprised.

There was a point that I had to get out more because I was starting to go stir crazy. I got together with my twin friends once a month at our twins meeting. Sometimes we would get together for play dates with our twins. At times we had six children together. We enjoyed watching our twins interact with each other.

The Mother of Twins organization was a support group for Mothers of Multiples. Twice a year the group had a clothing drive and you'd get to sell your baby items back or buy items. Once a year, we would attend the Mother of Twins convention, which was held in November. We looked forward to that weekend all year, a great way for moms to bonding together. There were some informative seminars for coping with multiples.

The conversations throughout the weekend were quite comical on the day-to-day challenges of raising twins at various ages. The majority agreed that it was 48 hours away from changing diapers.

The women whom I became friendly with we all our twins around the same time

I dressed the boys alike all the time. If one would spit up, I'd change both of them. I did not get that opportunity in the hospital to dress the boys, the way I intended.

Three and a half months of their lives was robbed from me, I was making up for all loss time that I missed. I wanted to be that mother of twins!

I just turned thirty years old in January of 1996. We had nothing planned. I was ecstatic to have two kids on my thirtieth birthday; I gave the boys a bath with them both sitting in the bathtub together. That was the best gift ever.

We knew the first birthday was around the corner, I pondered on the thought of how we all got here and how we are going to celebrate.

February 11, 1996, the boys' 1st birthday. We were skeptical of what we were going to do. February we can't be outside. We had this small house and we do not have the room for the family. Well, sure enough the night before the boys got sick, coughing, high fevers, and miserable.

I knew this was coming, as we were told in the hospital, the winter months were going to be tough on their lungs. The boys came down with RSV, (respiratory syncytial virus) which compounding side effect for premature babies and especially with chronic lung disease. Well, we can't forget the boys' birthday altogether. The boys had high fevers, with persistent coughing. We proceeded with the party. Later that night, the boys' symptoms had progressed. Their faces were bright red.

We meet with the pediatrician at his office that night and he confirmed, "They both have RSV." We were always worried about this virus. I felt guilty about having the first birthday party, but all we wanted was normalcy.

The pediatrician was concerned about the very high fevers the boys were developing. I though here we go we are going to the emergency room that night. The pediatrician prescribed the nebulizer, and if you're not familiar with the nebulizer. This is a breathing machine that can be used at home. Many children with asthma use this same machine. A dose of albuterol is added then can be administer. The child then breathes into the machine until the medicine is finished. These treatments open up the lungs and clear the lungs from infection. For the next two weeks, the boys had treatments three times a day, times two babies.

After the RSV diagnosis, I came upon another bizarre incident, every time I changed Matt's diaper.

Every time I would change him, I would have to press on his testicles to relieve his bladder. After a fearful amount of crying in the middle of the night, Matt's very hoarse cry led us to call the pediatrician. He instructed us to get Matt to the emergency room ASAP! This was our first emergency visit to CHOP. How is this going to work? Dave and I looked at each other in fear. Well, desperate times take desperate measures. We need to call a family member.

We calledl my mother and father-in-law, they came to their house to watch Tommy. Dave and I had to take Matt to the emergency room at CHOP. After a quick exam, the surgeon said, "The hernia is strangulated and we have to do the surgery now! If not, he's going to need a colostomy." This was our first encounter at CHOP. Of course, he had to stay in the hospital for at least forty-eight hours after that because of his medical history. The surgery went flawless l without complications.

We got to know the pediatric urologist from CHOP real quick. He got to really know my family over time and... then Tommy had a hernia operation a few months later. his hernia was not strangulated. This was a common procedure for preemies.

After the hernia surgeries, the boys were doing very well! We approached the springtime; the weather was getting warmer, longer days to bring the boys outside to play in the backyard, which their father redid for them. The grass was greener and healthier than anyone on our block. (It really looked like the greens at Pine Valley Golf Course). The boys loved to roll around on the grass with their cute little baby feet.

Life was pretty much business as usual. I decided at that point that I wanted to go back to work at least get one or two days back at the dental office. I had not worked for well over a year at this point, but the time felt much longer. I worked at a dental office Cherry Hill, NJ. I thought this would be therapeutic for me. The doctors were very excited with my decision to come back to the office, to work two days a week. We got the blessing from the pediatrician. Our family babysitter was thrilled for the opportunity to babysit this dynamic duo. Nicole was going to college at the time, and my schedule worked perfectly with hers....

Nicole really enjoyed caring for the boys. She was exhausted by the time I returned from the office. She said, "The boys are very active. How do you do this every day?" Everything was going well for a couple months, until my car accident. I was coming back from my twins' meeting and a car ran a stop sign and I landed right into a tree. My minivan was totaled. The boys' car seats were demolished. I hit a tree and I was rushed to the hospital. Dave was called to the scene, I was in a neck brace in an ambulance. (I had problems with my neck for a while from the accident. Working came to a complete halt. I didn't have a car to go anywhere because of the car accident After a few months of healing, I decided it would be best to ride out this storm and resume staying home with my dynamic duo!

We started looking in to our future plans as far as, job opportunities for Dave. After five years as an assistant golf course superintendent, at the most prestige golf course in the world. Dave wanted to set his sights on a course in the Pennsylvania area. We knew it was time to relocate our family for a better opportunity.

This was winter of 1996, when the Northeast was hit with a catastrophic "ice storm." Dave was interviewing in several counties of Pennsylvania and taking classes at Rutgers University. The boys and I were stuck in the entire winter, but I manage to put their "Eagles" snowsuits on and walk them around the block in the stroller.

The boys were two when we decided to relocate. The house in Cherry Hill was getting tight, and job opportunities were on the rise. After several interviews, Dave came back from the interview with pride and excitement. "There's a golf course in Bucks County Pennsylvania, which will be the future home of Lookaway Golf Club. I think this is the course that we have been looking for for quite some time now. The course is not built yet." It's nothing but dirt (aka soil) as a reference. I was happy for the great opportunity for Dave, but on the other hand, apprehensive that physically the course is in the planning stages.

Dave accepted the position at Lookaway Golf Club. We knew the change was going to be a game changer for us, as well as, the extended family members. The first response from family, "Why are you moving all the way to Pennsylvania?" The New Jersey folks had some mental block with the travel time of one hour. I think it was a bridge thing? We were getting excited for the move and a new beginning,

During the process of packing, I got a call from my Aunt Janice, with a melancholy tone in her voice, professing on how she was going to miss us. As stated previously, my aunt was always there when we needed her. Her support and thoughtfulness will never be forgotten, nor ever taken for granted.

The boys were active toddlers; they did not stop for two minutes. Matt would go east and Tommy would go west. Hence the name, "the dynamic duo"

"Everybody's going down to Sea Isle, New Jersey. Do you want to come?"

"All the cousins will be there?" she stated

I couldn't wait to get in the car. When I arrived to the shore house, the cousins were in awe of how I brought two of everything I needed for my "overnight stay." The family was perplexed and did not understood how my system worked. When you're by yourself taking care of two kids, you have a system.

I was a pro. I packed up the car when the boys were sleeping. I packed up the car and drove 2.5 hours down the shore. We had a blast and everybody was helping me out there. We went out that night and my uncle watched the kids. Finally, I'm having a good time. I didn't care how much work was involved. I didn't complain about how much time it took and what I needed to do. It was just what I needed for myself to get out.

We would go to the pediatrician and knew that the twins were not in the percentile of height and weight. The boys are alive and thriving. I kept saying to myself this was all worth it!

September of 1997 was when we moved to Pennsylvania. I remember my mom coming to the house on moving day, she was clearly very upset with me. She asked me, "Why was I doing this to her? How could you move away from your family?"

As the moving truck moved away, I said, "This is what we've got to do for us!" It has been a challenging two years, and we need a fresh start. We settled in this cute little house on the 11th hole at Lookaway Golf Course. The house needed some work, but we made it look really cute and it was perfect for just the four of us. At this point, the golf course was at the height of construction. The big dump trucks and excavators would be right in our back yard. I was afraid to bring the kids outside because of the dust storms. Let alone the safety for these little guys. Our yard was nothing but mud after a steady rain. I was stuck with these two kids and all they want to do is play in that mud! Of course, little boys live for mud. The ongoing reaction from everyone, "How can you live here?" I made it look adorable and we were happy.

We knew that something was going to come of this.

A few months after the move, I kneew something just didn't feel right inside me. I felt like I had something in my stomach. I've only been in Pennsylvania two months. I was driving on 611 going around and round and I didn't know how to get off the 611 by pass. Finally found the CVS, I purchased a pregnancy test, and I figured I take the test in the morning. I rose unusually early this morning, proceeding with the grogginess of morning, to find out the results indicated … the test was **positive**. I was elated, and super scared at the same time.

I thought to myself, *How am I going to tell Dave this news? How am I going to tell him this?* He was in the kitchen shuffling through the mail from yestrday and I said, "You got to sit down for this one," I said, "I'm pregnant," and he said, "How did that happen?" I said, "Do I really need to explain that?" He literally looked at me, didn't even say anything and walked out the back door.

I said, "Okay, that was great. I guess he didn't know how to react."

He came back a half hour later, "I thought we weren't going to have any more kids," I said, "This truly is a blessing. This is supposed to happen," Of course as I look back now, I was nervous at first knowing that I was pregnant but this was God's plan. I was supposed to be pregnant, another child.

Dave was very scared, but I guess me going through it, of course, I was scared. Dr. Mellen confirmed the pregnancy with an ultrasound later than week. July 4th was my due date for our new bundle. When I was fourteen weeks pregnant, Dr. Mellen decided on a surgical procedure to keep my cervix intact. There was no definite reason why the boys were born at twenty-four weeks, but Dr. Mellen want to take all the safety protocols with me. The only reasonable theory why I could not hold the twins was perhaps the cervix could not hold all the weight at five months pregnant.

At fourteen weeks pregnant I had the surgery. The procedure was called a cerclage, sutures were placed encircling of a malfunctioning cervix. After the procedure Dr. Mellen wanted me to be on bed rest for two weeks. I said to myself, "How is that going to happen." Luckily, we had some friends whom we meet in Buckingham. Our friends had three young daughters who were willing to take on the task of helping us out Kate and Kelly were eleven and twelve years old at the time. I was on so-called moderate bed rest with this pregnancy. How can one be on moderate bed rest with twins? The girls came over the first week after the surgery so I could rest while Dave was working. Dave was busy with the construction of the golf course. I got big pretty fast. I was sick for the first three months. I treasured those naps when Matt and Tommy were at the Tiny Tots Nursery School. I rapidly approached the twenty-four weeks landmark. I had some anxiety about the pregnancy and rightfully so. Dr. Mellen asked, "How are you feeling?" I said, "I don't think I'm getting contractions." I think it was more of a psychological then physical.

Out of extreme caution, Dr. Mellen put me on medication called Brethine. The medication keeps the uterus from contracting. The side effects of the medication led me to a rapid heart rate. The medication made me feel as if I was running a marathon all day. I had to take it every three to four hours. The morning sickness went away and I was starting to feel good. I was enjoying the cravings of friendly's ice cream, wow, this pregnancy was awsome. The success of the surgery and the medication gave me a sense of security. When I got to thirty weeks, wow! I'm almost there.

Thirty-seven weeks was my goal for this pregnancy! I knew from my previous pregnancy, that at thirty-seven weeks the lungs are fully developed. I couldn't wait any longer. I had to know the sex of the baby. I asked Dr. Mellen, to disclosed the sex of the baby. Dave didn't want to know the sex, and I never told him. This was my secret to myself. The boys were almost three and a half years old. They both knew another baby was coming. Why is mommy's belly so big? Tommy said, "How did you get fat so fast?" Tommy always had a way with words.

Dr. Mellen confirmed after his extensive exam, "Everything looks awesome."

I said, "Do I need to still take the Brethine?"

He said, "No, because you're thirty-seven weeks. His lungs are fully developed at this point you could go at any day now. Tuesday, I'll have you come in and we'll take the sutures out and then it's all fair game at that point." That night I couldn't sleep because I was getting contractions. After one missed dosage of the medication, I started getting contractions. I went downstairs and I was lying on the couch watching Conan O'Brien. After many hours of television, I went upstairs to wake up Dave. "I'm getting really bad contractions." I said, as tapped him on his shoulder. "Let's go to the hospital; I'm ready to give birth." We had to wait for Dave's brother to arrive at the golf course. Mike was working at the time at Lookaway. Mike wasn't a seasonal babysitter, let alone watching two kids at three years old.

Mike had one job, just make sure the boys don't go outside bury themselves in a pile of mud. Just keep them in one spot! Mike was going to bring the boys to Dave's parent's house later that afternoon. We got to Pennsylvania Hospital and I was pumped. I'm going to have a baby at full term. This is going to be the absolute bomb. The resident came in and said, "I'm going to take the sutures out now." I said, "Okay." Well, my God. The resident removed the cerclage sutures without any anesthesia!

After that ordeal, the resident alerts me, "You're not ready to go yet."

I said, "Well, we are not going all the way back to Bucks County! Let's go to your parent's house." Dave's parents lived thirty minutes from the hospital. We went back to his parent's house, while I was sitting on the couch timing the contractions. "She's getting a little closer with the contractions." Dave proceeds to call the hospital. The hospital knew that my previous pregnancy was a high-risk pregnancy, and we were so cautious throughout this pregnancy. At six o'clock that night we headed back to the hospital, with excitement! The joy had overridden those painful contractions. Dave's mom wanted to come. I was greeted in the lobby by one of the nurses, and instructed me that my room was ready. What?" Is this the Four Season Hotel? The orders from Dr. Mellen were a private room. In Dr. Mellen's jovial manner, "Jackie was getting the Presidential Suite this time! This is a time for celebration!

Dr. Mellen wanted to make sure everything was in place, since he was on call that weekend. His partner delivered this beautiful blonde hair, blue-eyed bundle of joy on June 13, 1998 at 10:10 p.m. Andrew came into our lives.

Andrew Gerard Renk, was one of happiest experience I had in such a long time. He was absolutely gorgeous. He came out absolutely perfect. Uncle Danny was there while I was being sutured, he proclaimed, "Jackie, he's beautiful and you were meant to have him." Everybody in my family was at the hospital. They were all sitting there waiting for Andrew's arrival.

Dave was there the whole time. If he was with me, he was watching *Cops* Every time "Cops" comes on now, Andrew says, "Oh, mom. Remember this show?"

The joy of having a full-term baby was clearly evident that anything can be possible with the assistance of modern medicine.

Incoming, I was greeted by Matt and Tommy. Both boys were proud to show off their matching tee shirts. "I'm the big brother. I'm the big brother," cute as a button with a cluster of balloons. Every cousin, were in attendance for Andrew's arrival. Everyone wanted to be there for the celebration. I had no physical pain because I was so elated. My pain was different and as I associated in this book that my pain was so deep from trauma that I have endured. Physical pain eventually goes away, but emotional pain has lasting scars.

I didn't sleep that whole night after the birth, I snuck out my room and I was MIA. I went down to the nursery. I just had a baby three hours ago. All I wanted to see was my baby in the nursery. The nurses came in.

"Where are you going?"

I said, "I'm going to go see Andrew right now."

She said, "You got to get back in bed," and I said, "I'm going to see him. You don't understand what this means to me. I have to go see my baby!"

"You need to get rest."

I said, "I'm not sleeping at a time like this. I feel like it's Christmas morning. I just had a baby. This is awesome." I had to explain to her my situation and she understood. I didn't sleep a wink.

"You really need to get sleep because you got to go back home to the twins." How is it hard? How is that hard from the standpoint of where I came from? This is a walk in the park. This is nothing, nothing of what I just went through a couple years ago.

The next day, Andrew was ready to come home from the hospital. I put this little outfit on, 'Dad's Little Slugger' Oh my God. His cheeks were just so delicious. I could not put him down for two seconds. Matt and Tommy's faces were so excited they had a little brother. The boys were so happy to see Andrew in the hospital. Dave took Matt and Tommy by the hand and brought them back down to the NICU to see the nurses who took care of them. The nurses were enthralled to see Matt and Tommy. Dave was a proud father of three boys now.

Back twenty-six years ago, the boys were the only twenty-four-week-old twins that were born, survived and had no residual issues. We knew that the boys would have some developmental delays. The initial grim prognosis was in the past for these miracle twins. Matt's brain bleed was resolved.

At fourteen months adjusted age, the adjusted age correlates to prematurity. The boys were born three and half months early. I don't recall if the physical therapist was at the house to witness this milestone, but I was there....

Matt was eighteen months at the time, and he standing next to the couch and all of a sudden, he walked over to me. The excitement that ran through my body was indescribable. When I think of that moment today, my smile is still the same. The diagnosis of cerebral palsy was null and void! These boys were truly a miracle, and I am grateful every day that I was chosen to take on this forever-challenging gift.

I called Dave at work and he was home in record timing....

Matt walked before Tommy. Tommy was a month later. I remember at Paulie's second birthday party, Matt was walking all over the place. Looking across the room, I saw my sister just burst into tears. I did not want to forget this huge milestone. In retrospect—Matt's diagnosis of cerebral palsy and never being able to walk. My sister was there to witness the diagnosis, which makes the outcome especially special.

Getting back to our new addition to the family. The elation of having this newborn and knowing there's a reason why we were blessed. Everyone would ask me are you ever going to put that baby down? Matt and Tommy were still at Tiny Tots, Nursery school three days a week. I was able to enjoy some quality time with Andrew. It's not hard with one baby, or maybe it's my perception. I've been through so much thus far; my perception of difficult times may be different than others.

Matt and Tommy were three and a half years old when Andrew was born. As we settled into our new lives with three boys, we needed to continue speech therapy with Matt. We found a therapist in the area. He was seeing the therapist twice a week and he was truly progressing at a rapid rate.

The big day finally arrived; The start of kindergarten for the twins. We decided that we were going to keep the boys together. The teacher was very accommodating to the boys and their dynamic personalities. In the middle of the school year, the teacher asked me, "Were the boys born pre-mature?" and I said, "Yes. Why do you ask?" She replied, "I have observed their developmental delays. If a child is developmentally delayed 33 1/3, they're eligible for early intervention, but they weren't delayed to that de-gree. Of course, as a first-time mother, you listen to the kindergarten teacher, and she suggested to send them to first grade. I didn't know if they were ready for first grade, which in hindsight I should have kept them back in kindergarten. Both boys had IEPs, individual educational program. The IEPs were in place throughout their grade school years.

Tommy was having many episodes of sleep apnea, irritable all the time and at times he would choke while he was eating. We went back to Children's Hospital for a tonsillectomy. Tommy had to stay two nights be-cause of his medical history and he wasn't the best patient, but we got through that surgery...

The decision to separate the boys in first grade was rather tough deci-sion on all of us for many emotional reasons.

That was a tough decision for me because I finally separated them. They were both in different classes. The separation was a blessing for the boys because they both actually started flourishing with their identity.

They both latched on to friends. They still had their twin friends. Tommy dressed which best suited his personality, and Matt followed in his own unique way as well. The back-to-school nights were challenging to budget my time equally in each classroom. Andrew was three years old at this point and he started nursery school. I needed to go back to work part-time I started out one evening and a Saturday at a dental office in Doylestown. I needed to meet people and have some adult conversation, besides mimicking all the lyrics to Barney. I had a little apprehension at first, because I have not worked in several years. Only that short-lived time in Cherry Hill, New Jersey. While living on the golf course was a great experience for the boys, for me it presented a challenging way to meet friends. Working turned to be a wonderful transition.

Motherhood has been the most rewarding title one-can possess in a life-time....

The challenges and rewards that has been presented to me thus far, outweighs the negatives attributes associated with my journey in this book.

I guess I don't see the world like most do. I could never understand the trivial aspects of life...Some Mothers complaining about how "HARD IT

IS TO BE A MOM" Perhaps, it may be a coping mechanism for some. I never saw myself as a complainer, or the one thinks that the world owes me because of my traumatic experiences, which I hold in my heart forever I often think, I wish I was playing golf with my son again. Just to have one more day with him. I wish I had just a little more time. Difficult as it may sound; playing golf today gives me the constant reminder of how precious our lives are. Every time I take my nine iron out of my bag, I think of best bonding that I had with Matt. My bag tells a story how this game with my son came to fruition. This golf bag, by far, is one of my most cherished possessions which I own. Matt started off by buying me the bag (with help from his father) "Mom, you need new clubs because these clubs are crap," and demanding to go get more clubs. Each Mother's Day for the past eight years, I got a new club for my bag. Every time I pick up one of those clubs that he gave me, it brings me back to the sanctity of the game. Golf has been an interwoven part of my life. Golf is a game, which can be played at seven years old until seventy-seven years old.

When Matt first came to me, "Mom, would you want to play golf?" He was seven years old at the time.

When we came to Lookaway, I was very busy with raising our sons. I loved being on the golf course but I didn't have the time until Matt's askd me to play at seven years old. "Mom, do you want to play golf with me?" Every Monday afternoon at five o'clock, we played a couple holes after work. I would pull up in the driveway, my clubs were out on the driveway, shoes placed next to the bag, and golf cart backed up ready to go. The bonding I had with my son while we were playing was extraordinary.

Back to February 11,2015

As the day went on, the bittersweet emotions that I have on this day will never leave me. Tommy was stressed out and bewildered after he got home that afternoon. "Are you ready?" he said in stern tone. We all got into the truck, on this cold February afternoon drove over to the first hole at Lookaway I gave him the package of ashes which I preserved for moments like these. He opened up the plastic bag and sprinkled his brother's ashes on the first Tee box. He wanted to do this for their twentieth Birthday. My heart just melted to the ground. We all had a moment of silence for about five minutes we could only hear the crackling of the wind against the trees. Today was just the four of us. This moment was absolutely sacred. The maturity and acceptance of the past came to Tommy and Andrew's expressive emotions. Every time I play the first hole at Lookaway, the emotions run through my spine and struggle to play this hole. Now the course has become a special place in my heart.

This course has become a place that I could cry, scream and reflect on what happened here. We raised our three boys. The boys have been at the course all of their lives. Lookaway is a special place for us. It's more of a place where we raised our family and most of my adult life has been at this nostalgic and majestic golf course. So many wonderful memories to cherish at this home. However: some profound trauma has been interwoven with those fond memories. As I move forward with my journey of Motherhood my appreciation for the smaller little things in life trumps nothing else in the world.

Tommy has come a long way, a very long way from where he was just a few years prior. I've seen the maturity and respect for his twin brother. It shouldn't be on your twentieth birthday that you're spreading your brother's ashes. It just shouldn't be. Andrew deals with the loss in a way that he tries to break the silence. He may crack a joke or jump all to the pond and see if the pond is frozen. Andrew always has a way to make light of the situation. That's his way of dealing with pain.

Over the years, watching Tommy not having his brother and all the other milestones which one may share with their twin brother, going to the prom, graduating from high school, and entering college, or the work force. For me as a mother, the agony of observing these lost milestones is a constant reminder of what could have been for us. Every day is tough, but the celebration of Tommy's birthday and the constant reminder of the loss of the twin bonding can never be replaced. I salute Tommy on his strength the way he honored Matt, so eloquently with his presentation was just incredible.

Andrew looked up to his brothers so much, as any younger brother would in birth order. Matt always took care of Andrew. Matt loved feeding a bottle to Andrew when Matt was a tot himself. Matt was just always compassionate towards his brothers, as well as, any human being. He was the type of kid when you said, "Matt, can you go do this for me?" he would answer, "Sure, Mom." He never gave me a hard time about anything.

As I expressed there's many scars in my life. In writing this memoir, the scabs are ripped off again, and the bleeding starts all over again. I think this journey has given me the strength to bleed again. Writing has been therapeutic for me. By no means has language arts been my strong suit.

Pursuing a feared and complex mission, in itself, has been a remarkable accomplishment in my life. I felt the need to invite people on my journey, not out empathy, but to understand that life can be unimaginable and out of control. I just had to keep moving on. All of my sons have taught me to move on. I think it's just so important for others to understand you just can't say why me??? If I had to take this journey again, I would do it all over and what I learned as a person, and the strength, which I've gained along the way. The little joyful moments: Matt taking his first steps, Matt and Tommy cooing at each other, Andrew being born, seeing all three boys together playing car wash in the cozy coup. Those are the days that I cherish because it gets me through the trauma.

Middle School Years....

It was the spring of Seventh grade when Matt and Tommy were walking down the driveway, Tommy said, "Mom, Matt threw up on the bus." I was not real concerned with the incident because it probably something that he ate at school.

Later that evening Matt came out of the family room and projectile vomited all over the floor. Of course, he apologized.... I did call the pediatrician that evening and told him that he was having headaches and throwing up. Pediatrician suggested that if the vomiting continued to take him to the ER.

That whole weekend Matt was just not himself; I knew something was just not right. The next day Matt was getting ready for school, came into the kitchen and throw up his Fruity Pebbles all over the kitchen floor. "Okay, get your shoes on we are going to the hospital." I demanded. At the time, Dave was at the bus stop with Andrew and Tommy. I Stopped and told him that we were headed to the hospital and that I call him as soon as I knew what was going on.

As I entered the hospital, the nurses took him back as soon as they could. Within forty-five minutes, I got the worst news a mom could ever hear.... "Your son has a brain tumor." Confirmed with a CT scan. The crippling news leads me on the floor of Doylestown hospital. I remember a few people asking me if I was okay? As I started to regain my thoughts, I started calling as many people as I could. Nobody seemed to answer his or her phone! Within time, Dave called me back, I told him to get here NOW! Just get here....

In the meantime, Matt was lying in the hospital bed not know what just happened. I just could not bear to lose it right now with him. I needed to be strong for him.

The attending physician told me that we needed to get Matt to the Children's Hospital of Philadelphia ASAP! I remember getting into the hot ambulance, it was 102 degrees that day; Dave followed us in his truck in to Philadelphia. Matt was in the back watching *Monsters Inc*. He was so calm, probably because of the pain medication given in his IV.

We eventually arrived at CHOP, so overwhelmed with the ER running around and trying to get Matt settled in a room for examination.

Within in an hour or two, one of the physicians told us that neurologist need to see the both of us in his office now.

Dave and I were both trying to find the office. We were walking around in a daze and asking everyone where is the neurologist's office? As we entered the office, the doctor was sitting there waiting for us. He rambled on about this and that, I couldn't comprehend anything he was stating to us. All I remember was what he told us that our son had a brain tumor and the tumor was hemorrhaging, He said, "The surgery is scheduled for tomorrow at 7:30 a.m."

Dave and I just stared.... The doctor stated that the tumor was a medullablastoma, which is the posterior fossa of the head (the back portion of his head). The doctor further suggested, if we wanted a second opinion, you don't have much time. With all of that to digest, we walked backed to the ER, dazed and confused. A typical day ended up in a life-altering situation. We walked back to the room and low and behold the entire family was by Matt's bedside. My dad brought Andrew and Tommy to the hospital, and they were in SHOCK. Matt asked, "Pop, am I going to die?" How is someone supposed to answer that question? I stayed in the hospital that night with Matt; Dave brought Andrew and Tommy home. They would be returning by 6:00 a.m. for the surgery. Well, they were back at 4:00 a.m., because no one could sleep that night.

Matt was taken into pre-op area, and the thoughts that went through my mind, "Will my son survive?" He will never be the same child again after brain surgery. The surgery took over seven hours, and we all waited in the waiting area. The doctor came out and told us "your son has brain cancer." I just knew he was gonna say that! I freaked out and ran right to the bathroom. All of this was a lot to process in less than forty-eight hours.

My knees buckled with my hands in in my face. Why? How could of this happened so fast?

Matt was in ICU for four weeks with many struggles, Hydrocephalus (brain swelling), hallucinations, infections, and lack of any sort of communication to us.

Within a week, he had a VP shunt placed to reduce the swelling in his brain.

He was later brought to the oncology floor, where Andrew and Tommy brought their brothers belongings in a wagon. Andrew asked innocently to the nurse, "Why are all the rooms decorated with kid stuff?" The nurse said to Andrew, "The children who come to this floor are here for a long time, and we decorate their rooms so they feel like they are home." Andrew's face of innocent despair was heartbreaking to witness. As we settled into Matt's new home, we all had many questions that have built up over these past weeks? Will Matt walk, talk, eat, write, or have any resemblance prior to the surgery?

We finally meet Matt's oncologist for the first time. She was very a matter of fact. We had to talk about rehab, radiation, chemotherapy, and the next six months of his life. WOW, that's a lot to digest....

The oncologists thought that Matt could come home for the weekend before Rehab, OT, PT, Speech, and radiation would start. Matt was discharged on the July 4 weekend and everybody came to the house to support him on his long journey ahead. Monday morning, we started the rehabilitation at Children's Seashore house. We started Occupational, Speech, Physical therapy, and radiation.

We went back to school in September for only one month.

We made the decision that we wanted him to show his face to the eighth-grade class because when he left seventh grade he was vomiting at school. That whole summer of seventh grade was blown up due to diagnosis and treatment. We met with the principal, all his teachers to inform the safety precautions with Matt coming back to school. His balance was way off and his appearance was not quite the same, when he left in June. He would need a pass and assistance going to his classes. He had a key to the elevator and a guide if needed. We wanted him to experience eighth grade, at least partial, because we know he was going to start chemo in October. His chemotherapy protocol indicated that his hospital stays would be approximately six months.

It was great to have Matt home for the weekend, but the challenges were insurmountable: I had to follow him around the house like a fifteen-month-old, because his balance was way off, and he kept falling. The steroids made him blow up like a blowfish. We had some friends and family over to see Matt.

Matt started eighth grade that September, with his doo-rag on his head to cover his "baldness" not a stitch of hair on his head. After day one, he came back in the kitchen He did want to have any provisions that his appearance was different. He was strong. He said, "I'm not taking the elevator. I'm going to take the classes and I'm going to walk through the hall like everybody else," he stated sternly, pulling his hat off his head. He didn't want to be treated special. After that outburst, we started calling Matt, IRON MAN.

Matt was diagnosed on June 6, 2008 and then he was discharged from the hospital July 4 weekend. He was in ICU for four weeks. Before radiation we discuss with the team that he would be sterile after thirty-three rounds of radiation. That was another decision we had to make that my son would not be able to be a father.

Of all people to be a father. Really?

Radiation started my PTSD! The emotion pain of seeing my son go through such intense treatment never goes away. The visions are engrained in my mind for the rest of my life. The vision can be hidden with therapy, but the trauma never leaves. A part of my life that was extremely traumatic, but I have to find a way to get to a place that you can function each day. I have to learn how to function on my own. No one knows the travesty of **walking in my shoes**.

When I think about radiation I get chills. Radiation therapy was far more barbaric for a mother to watch than no other. The very thought of my son's brain radiated each day for 33 rounds was a lot of one human being to digested, let alone to watch.

The emotionally impact which the mask left me. The construction of the mask was of mesh formation that fit over his face in a secure manner. The first time I saw the mask, I nearly threw up. Of course, I needed to bury that emotion, because I needed to be Strong! I did speak to the radiation oncologist in length of why such a confining mask? He stated, "We need to keep Matt perfectly still while we radiate his brain, and we need to do a "power boost" to the posterior fossa where the tumor was present.

While I am writing the details in this book, the Tsunami comes back in full force. I can't get the mask out of my mind.

Years later, Andrew was preparing a PowerPoint project. The project was to describe a traumatic experience in his life. Andrew came to radiation the one time with Tommy. Andrew described that seeing his brother going through radiation was his most traumatic experience. He needed to show pictures of radiation. We were both working at the kitchen table sorting through pictures of radiation. He showed me a picture of patient getting ready for radiation treatment, with the mask on. "Oh my God!" I screamed in terror, "Don't show me that picture," I said rather abruptly. I had to walk out of the room.

The wave of stress and fear was so intense that the anxiety attack lead me to a tsunami, the moment was so profound.

Matt was supposed to start getting sick two weeks after radiation. He got sick the first day of radiation. Coming home from CHOP that afternoon, one of the guys from the golf course made this great dinner for Matt. It was lobster tail with all, the fixings. We all sat down ready to eat and within ten minutes it was all over the porch. We all got up, Andrew went to get the bucket, Tommy would get the hose to wash the vomit away. I'd go get Matt a new shirt. We just all were like roaches knowing what our duties were. This was the Renk Family new normal We just got used to our new normal over time.

Matt was one of the first pediatric patients to receive treatment at the new facility across from CHOP, The University of Pennsylvania Hospital. Every day we would head across the street for radiation. On this particular day, one of the security guards stopped Matt and I and he said "Hey, buddy, keep fighting the fight!" Wow, that was a burst of confidence that was very well needed.

We were going back and forth to CHOP every day for the entire month of August. We all agreed as a family, that going back and forth to CHOP each day was the best treatment option for Matt's rehabilitation. There were many modalities which Matt need for recovery: Speech, occupational, and Physical therapies.

The opposing treatment option was in patient stay at the Children's Seashore House, which was across the street from the main hospital.

Children's Seashore House was a phenomenal place, but seeing those children made an impact on Matt. We visited the facility before discharge, and Matt did not want any part of staying in the hospital for another month. The children were not just there for a week, a month; Some patients are there for years. Some of those kids are never coming home. Keeping those emotions to myself totally ripped my heart out.

The option to travel back and forth to the hospital was the better of two evils. The hour and twenty minutes every day was better than the inpatient stay. We would stay at CHOP all day long with the therapies and ended the day with radiation... and I just want to clarify. It wasn't that ride. It was the emotional drain. It was the emotional drain of watching my son struggle to regain his life back. The most annoying question I got each day, "How do you drive back and forth to the hospital each day?" I did that when he was born, and I am doing it again. I never even thought about the travel. I was just trying to make my son better and I'd do it at any cost. Today if I had to do it all over again, I would in a heartbeat!

Throughout radiation, Tommy was very inquisitive on what was happening to Matt and how he could help him with his road to recovery.

I knew Tommy was pretty troubled because he kept talking about radiation and all of Matt's therapies.

Dave and I thought It may be a good idea that Tommy and Andrew both came to the hospital to give Matt some support with his therapies. I felt like this particular day would be tolerable because we had something to look forward to that night. It was that night we were going to the Phillies game.

Again, Tommy was only thirteen years old at the time. Andrew was ten, not quite sure what was happening to Matt. Both boys were too young to go through this traumatic experience. Watching their brother going through brain surgery. Matt's Post op complications: not able to recall events, not be able to talk, walk, and eat, unable to tie his shoes.

We started out with speech therapy. Matt was putting words together and he started to comprehend. He was getting back. He was getting back to all the rehab that he had since the surgery. His occupational therapists were amazed. Tommy was so active in this session.

The therapists were teaching Matt how to write with his left hand because he had tremors from the surgery. The boys were doing strength training on the hand bike. I was pleased to see dynamic duo getting back together. They've been separated since June 7" the day of Matt's surgery. The boys really did not see Matt too much. Andrew loved hanging out with his big brothers; the bonding was incredible the way they were reacting towards each other. After occupational therapy it was time for some fun.

The boys were active with Matt doing push-ups, and walking on the treadmill in physical therapy. The therapist suggested a little one-on –one with the boys. We went to roof top segment of seashore house and they were all playing basketball together. I had such a huge smile to see all three boys together again.

The only word I can describe going down to radiation every day was walking the Green Mile, trying to put one foot in front of the other walking down that hallway, and knowing that my son's brain was going to be radiated today.

The treatment took about 45 minutes to an hour, but it felt like days. It felt like days because they have to set him up, adjust the settings, and put the mask on. He could not move. Tommy said to me, "Mom, I'm ready to go back to be with Matt." So, I said, "Okay, let's go." I said to, Andrew, "Just wait here. I'll be back." We went back to the treatment area, I was a lot more nervous for Tommy, than for myself.

Do I allow them to come back and see what was going on? Tommy asked me, "I need to go back in radiation. I need to go back and be with Matt." I just didn't know, he's only thirteen this kid's been through enough trauma already. Do I allow him to see this? Matt wasn't just going into an MRI machine. This was more barbaric than I have ever seen in my life. He was lying on the table with a mask on his face all locked in. I turned to look at Tommy's face expression, and he was white as a ghost. He looked like he was going to pass out. I was praying for this to be over fast.

The day finally came to end. Now it's time to enjoy a night at the Phillies game. We stayed at Holiday Inn over on Packer Avenue next to the stadium. We all needed to have a breather from CHOP. Matt went downstairs to the lobby to buy his own Phillies jersey. I'll never forget. It was blue and red jersey. We all had our Phillies game day Gere on. Dave came to pick us up at the Holiday Inn, we went to the game. Dave informed me that this night was going to be a special Night! Dave knew the superintendent at the Citizen's Bank Park. He gave us a special preview of the stadium and we were able to go on the field. Matt wanted to see all the John Deere equipment. He was more excited about seeing the equipment than being on the field. The most captivating part of that night, which kind of validates how respectful Matt was as a young man. I knew he was something else. At the beginning of the game, the "National Anthem." He stands up and takes his hat off with not a stitch of hair on his head and puts his hand on his heart and just starts singing. I thought that was honorable. He stood up in front of everybody ...

He said, "I really don't care. I'm going to respect this country, and that's what I was taught all my life." That was absolutely incredible and I just never forget looking at him. This kid is really something else. Are you kidding me?

In Treatment 27, we had six rounds of radiation to go. This is almost over; There was light at the end of this dark tunnel! As we were approach our last day of radiation, my dad wanted to take Matt to his last treatment. Dad called me and said, "When Matt is done with radiation, I am going to take him down to our shore house." Dad insisted. My dad wanted to give me a break. "You're not going to go to treatment today, I'm going to take care of all of it." I met my dad on I95, at Matt's favorite place, Dunkin Donuts. We started a ritual after treatment each day. We stopped off at Dunkin Donuts as we approached our exit off of I95. He got two donuts, 1 jelly, 1 cream donut and large French vanilla Coffee Cool Atta. I didn't know how that all mixed in, but it worked for Matt. Dad took Matt down the shore and I said, "Oh, this is great. We got through radiation!" Dave and I went down to the house, the very next day.

This house was my dad's parent's house which we spent many summers there as kids.

My mom passed away at fifty-seven years old to heart disease. My mother was a chain smoker, with many emotional issues.

The boys called my dad Pop. Pop spoiled Matt with many gifts from the local beach store, with a new boogie board, and a plethora of new clothes. My dad just thoroughly enjoyed just spending the time with Matt by himself.

As my Dad greeted us at the front door, he called me to the side asked to speak to me privately. As Pop tried to express himself in his uncontrollable tears, "Jackie, I do not know how you got through radiation, that was the most horrible experience I ever endeavored. "Everyone needs to walk through the halls of CHOP, to really appreciate their lives."

Now, I understand what it means to be emotionally drained. One may be physically drained, but when you're emotionally drained it does take a toll on your body.

I left the house at seven o'clock in the morning and would not get home till 5:30 every day, five days a week.

From what I remember our neighbors would drop meals off every night. That was a godsend. I wasn't really thinking, the family just got used to what was happening. All four of us were in different directions. I was with Matt all the time. Andrew was occupied with his baseball. Tommy was trying to be with friends. I felt like I was an absentee mother. I felt like I was pulled in so many directions and I was trying to do so much. Andrew would say to me, "You know, you do have two other children," The family in disarray left Andrew very confused.

An intricate part of the whole process was that Dave and I were still a team! Dave trying to keep the golf course alive, during a very hot summer, and keeping the boys busy. Everybody tried to help out as far as that aspect. The dynamics of the family was blown up. That hot June day changed the dynamics of this close-knit family. We had the Norman Rockwell painting that was blown up in flames, and never get that image back. We got through prematurity, had a new addition, Andrew. Things were going well for us. Then we are thrown into this heartache. I would often say to myself what did I do to deserve this? Look you're a strong person; I don't know how you do it? Was I offered plan B? Walking in these tight, worn out shoes, that I would never want anyone to even try on, let alone borrow. No awards are given out for this one. The final consult for chemotherapy:

Neuro-Oncology team explained the extensive treatment, the risks and complications associated with the medications, and the side effects with propose to possible secondary cancers. Thinking in my mind, oh, we're going to have this poison injected into our son's body and then and everything's going to be fine?" I felt as though I had no voice in the conversation. I just have to agree to the treatment plan. My son has brain cancer, what's the alternative? I had to sign a twenty-page consent. The hospital stays were going to be long. I needed to get Matt his ammunition up to fight this battle.

Matt's protocol for (chemotherapy treatment) was St. Jude's protocol for pediatric brain cancer. Treatment protocol came from St. Jude's hospital in Tennessee.

ROUND ONE OF CHEMOTHERAPY

It's time to check in to our new home for the next six months...

As we enter the first round of chemo, we have some idea of what is about to take place, but no idea of the physical demand that this protocol will take on my son's body.

Chemotherapy was absolutely exhausting. As we settled in to this unknown world, I was thinking to myself, this couldn't be as horrible as radiation? Chemo didn't start till late that night. By the time we got him situated, the drugs came via pharmacist. Every drug was administered in a specific sequence. All through the night, the drugs kept coming and coming. When was this madness going to end?

We were nestled in this small room in the corner of the Oncology floor. I never closed my eyes that evening, because of the foot traffic in Matt's room. The next day Matt gets out of bed, and starts walking around the oncology floor with his Mayo stand carrying his sodium chloride. I said to him, "where do you think you are going?" He replied, "Can't I take a walk?" I guess the drugs last night did not faze him one bit. I thought to myself, if the next four rounds were going to be this uneventful for him, then I'll be okay. Approximately three or four days later his counts dropped.

That's normal for chemotherapy for your white blood cells to go to zero.

We were both sitting in this little room watching the Phillies game; This particular game was game 2 of the World Series. The Phillies won the World Series in 2008. A historical event to be watching in a hospital room, let alone stationed in the heart of Philadelphia. As we sat together, I said, "How do you feel?" He said "Okay," I said, "I'm going to take you somewhere." He said, "What?" I took him out of the hospital because he was not connected to an IV. We went down the elevator and across the street to Potbelly. This sandwich place had the best milkshakes. I said, "Let me go get you a milkshake." He said, "Mom, I can't believe you are doing this," I said, "You know what? Sometimes in life you just got to do it." This kid was so excited to get back to his room to call his father, to tell on his mother. He said, "Dad, you won't believe what Mom just did. She just took me out of the hospital, and I don't know if the nurses knew we left. I can't believe that she did that! I got a milkshake from Potbelly's."

I wanted Matt to feel some sort of normalcy, in a very controlled situation.

ROUND TWO-

It was the middle of November when we started round two of chemo. First round was a little bit longer getting back to the hospital because we had to wait until his white blood cells started to come up. Matt's cells were preserved before chemotherapy, with a process called Apheresis. He was going to be in the hospital for Thanksgiving. Our lasts thoughts at this round were where are we going to have Thanksgiving dinner?

We were admitted to an even smaller room than last round. Dave was with me this time. I said to Dave, "You have to be here to experience what's going to happen. This is really tough and I can't do this by myself, at least the first drug." I knew that first drug was the toughest for Matt, as well as, me to witness. Again, waiting hours upon hours, waiting for the drugs to come down from pharmacy.

Dave and I were in the room. The boys were my sisters' house because I know the first day of chemo was always tough. It was always tough for me because now I had the first round under my belt. I knew what to experience.

We were trying to keep Matt occupied before the drugs came. I was trying to relax myself, but that was next to impossible. Not even mediation, could prepare you for this first drug. The vincristine was administered into the IV. Within one minute, Matt was coughing, gasping for breath, turning blue, and projectile vomiting started like I never have seen! Dave just looked at me and said, "Oh my God. Oh my God. Now I know what you're talking about,"   Dave stayed most of the night, until most of the drugs were administered, and Matt seemed to be calmer. As soon as Dave left, this night was a night that I wouldn't forget.

Matt was in the bed.

He was not asleep at this point. It was in the middle of the night.

When you're in the hospital for long hospital stays with your child, you're doing a lot of work. I cleaned up diarrhea and vomit constantly. The nurses were great. The parent gets the child through the emotion piece. Around 3:30 a.m. Matt started hallucinating, and he started going into convulsions. I thought I was going to lose him. He was smashing things. I was calling for the nurses.

Finally, the nurses came running in. I said, "You need to calm him down." He was trying to get out of the bed. He was freaking out. I said, "What is happening to my son?" "It's the drugs. It's the chemotherapy." I said, "Why is he hallucinating?" and they said, "Don't worry, Mom. It's just the drugs," "You got to do something. Can you just calm him down a little bit? He's torn the entire room apart. I never seen him react like that before. Why is this happening? The convulsions scared the hell out of me." I know I'm going to lose my son tonight. I'm here alone again dealing with this by myself.

The next morning Matt's nurse said, "We got a bigger room for Matt, we will be moving him into another room. I said, Perhaps, a room will a window?" I mean, really there were no windows in this room. It was horrible. The staff was very apologetic. I was delirious at this point. I'm going on day three and haven't slept in two days. I was still reflecting on the last night horror. We eventually were moved into the big room. Dave and the boys came to visit Matt later than evening. "Oh, good. You got a cool room. We can actually move in this room." Andrew replied in relief. Matt wanted to change the room around. He wanted put the bed in a different location. "Well, I'm going to be here long enough," He stated in sarcastic tone. Dave took one look at me, "You need to go home, your eyes are blood shot, and you are staring into space."

I was going into day four of chemo. I said, "I need a break!" Dave agreed to stay the night with Matt.

I took the car back home with the boys. Driving home the boys were inquisitive, asking me a battery of questions. "Why does this have to happen to our family?" Andrew stated in an angry voice. Later that evening, Andrew asked to come stay in my bed with me. "Mom, are you okay?" "Yeah, I'm going to be okay," I couldn't really sleep because I was worried about what was going at the hospital. As soon as I feel asleep, the phone rang. It was Matt. He said "Mom, you better come back tomorrow, because Dad does not know what the hell he is doing!" I just needed one night in my own bed.

Andrew's grade school teachers got together and donated a Thanksgiving dinner for our family. We were grateful for gesture, but little did the teachers know that we were going to be at the hospital for Thanksgiving. We gave the Thanksgiving dinner to my family so they can enjoy it. The delicious meal was from Wegmans. We knew that meal was going to be great. Andrew and Tommy had their Thanksgiving dinner from the Oncology family room. Most of the families gathered around to share their meal with their loved ones as well. The sight saddens me that both boys were eating on their laps on paper plates. Tommy did turn and said, "Mom this meal sucks! Why can't we just be home?"

Matt barely ate. He wanted more to be home with his family, and not stuck in a hospital room.

Chemo patients usually have a bad metallic taste in their mouths. The taste buds are diminished, the sense of smell and taste lands into an aggressive state of vomiting. As we finished the second round, I started to observe the drastic weight loss and strength. The effects from the chemo were changing my son.

We were approaching the beginning of December. We had to go back to the clinic for a spinal tap A spinal tap for Matt, was a walk in the park. He would lie there perfectly still. He did glance over at me, and say" Why are you staring at me? I'm gonna be fine Mom!" After the spinal tap, we needed to head to the main hospital for a three-hour MRI. The MRI confirmed that the scan was clear, and no cancer cells present!

As we were driving home from CHOP, ecstatic from Matt's MRI results, Matt said, Mom It's time to get ready for Christmas!"

I said, "Really?" Matt loved Christmas. If you ever recalled the movie *The Polar Express*? The little boy in the movie was Matt. It was so amazing how much he loved Christmas. He loved the family getting together with his cousins. We were between rounds, and Matt was home schooled. The teachers would come, once or twice that week. Of course, there was a small window of opportunity, depending on how Matt was feeling that particular day. I said, "What do you want to do today?" He said, "We need to get the house ready for Christmas!" I will be home for Christmas, I am not going back in the hospital!" My suggestion, "Well, let's go shopping," of course, I bought everything I tiouched for Matt during this time. First stop was Eastern Mountain Sports; Matt was trying on work boots, jackets, gloves, and hats. After that large purchase, we were on to the next stop. I felt this was a time for Matt to enjoy his time with me, because he may not be with us next year. We still have three more rounds of chemo in front of us. My whole mantra was to celebrate this very moment. As we pulled in the parking lot of Target, Matt said," Mom Thanks for taking care of me."

It was not the materialistic part of the day; Matt knew the emotional drain of his treatment was taking a toll on me. He knew I kept my emotions inside. As we walked into Target, I said, Matt, we are going to need two shopping carts for this trip." He was so excited. We got these two 5 ft. angels, three reindeer, boxes and boxes of lights, Christmas decorations, and lots of sweet treats. We could not see in front of us as we approached the cash register.

Matt and I bought every Christmas decoration that you could imagine. I was determined to make this a great Christmas for Matt. I had a feeling that he may not be at home for Christmas, but I was going to do? As soon as we got home from Target, he was on his golf cart to put up all the decorations outside. I peered out from the front window, and just cried my eyes out on the sitting room couch. I thought to myself this torture that this young man has gone through thus far, and we still have a great deal more.

Dave walked into the kitchen and said, "Are you kidding me? He's outside putting the decorations up?" I said, "Oh, yeah." That's Matt!

Third round of chemo was approaching quickly. We had an appointment with Matt's Oncologist and the team shortly after his counts came up. The oncology team came in and said, "Matt, we got to talk to you." and he said, "What?" In a very reserved approach, they told him that going to be in the hospital for Christmas.

He got very upset. I never have seen him this upset. He wasn't disrespectful. He walked out of the room, and kept walking. He got angry. "This isn't fair," and he's right. It's not fair.

He was remotely upset crying and crying, "Mom, I can't believe this. We're going to be here for Christmas." I said, "Oh, God. Thank Goodness we decorated the house. We were going to make best of what we can for the next few days.

We started the third round knowing what we were in for.

As we approached the clinic for check-in, I said to the charge nurse, "Can I take this round for Matt?" Her reply, Mom, I know watching you son go through these rounds and rounds of chemo are next to impossible." At least I got some reassurance that I was not going crazy.

We had a consultation with the dietician, before we started the third round. She was adamant about Matt gaining weight. Matt needed to consume this exorbitant amount of calories in one day. Her goals were unrealistic. Her and I bucked heads on many occasions! Well, my philosophy was to give the patient what he/she could tolerate. He ate pasta practically every night when he was home. He just never ate when he was in the hospital. If he wants a bag of Doritos for breakfast, and he kept it down for twenty minutes it was a good day. She proceeds with the horrific threats of the nasogastric tube, (NG). This is a flexible tube of rubber or plastic that is passed through the nose, down through the esophagus, and into the stomach. Just a conversation of the tube placement in his nose, made him angry. We were not going to have an almost fourteen-year-old walking around with a tube in his nose. We were going to fight that conversation. Matt was on a very high dose of Zofran, which is an anti-nausea medicine that he took four times a day, but still got sick anyway.

Matt developed an infection called C-diff, right after we started chemo. This infection promotes life-threatening diarrhea. He had so many diarrheas that his behind was raw. I had to use Desitin and put a diaper back on him again. I know he was embarrassed that his mother was changing him, but in the grand schemes of things, what else could happen?

I said, "Oh, this is great." He's in the hospital for Christmas and he's got a life-threatening infection.

Matt wasn't allowed to leave the room. He had to stay in quarantine to this room.

Well, I said to Matt, guess what? Christmas is going to be here. I'm going to make the best of it. I wanted to put a tree his room to cheer him up. I said, "Let's put a tree outside your room so all the other kids can enjoy the tree." I marched down to the CVS, which was only a block away. CVS was part of my daily ritual during rounds. I was running down Thirty-Third Street with four bags of ornaments, and a Christmas tree!

I came back from CVS. I said, "Matt, look, I brought decorations."

"*Awe*, Mom. That's great. Mom, you're awesome." I tried my best that I can to make this little boy get through his favorite holiday. I asked one of the nurses "where would be the best place to put the tree?" She said, Mrs. Renk, you are something else! You are going to light up this whole Oncology floor." I remembered there was a little girl down the hall that coded the night before. The parents were in the hallway and I said, "How are you doing?" and the father said, "We just lost our daughter." I stood in shock, lost for words. I noticed that beautiful artwork that was her door. I said, "Did you draw that beautiful picture of Santa Clause?" He said, "I sure did!" "Do you have a son or daughter here?" he asked. "What's his name, and what does he like?' "He loves trucks," I said. "He loves John Deere." Sure enough, the next day I woke up and he had the John Deere logo on Matt's window. Matt woke up and asked, "What's that?" I said, "A dad down the hall was drawing logos on all the kids' doors." I didn't tell him the whole story because I was wiped out. I'm just emotionless, after what those parents down the hall just told me. I thought to myself, those parents could be Dave and I.

Dave came in moments later, to relieve me from my shift.

I needed to go home to go Christmas Shopping for Andrew and Tommy wrap their presents and head back to the hospital. All Andrew and Tommy wanted was their brother to be home for Christmas. There was an organization at the hospital that came in and asked us, what does Matt want for Christmas? And I remember it was Matt wanted the iTouch.

Matt just wanted his life back. He wanted to live cancer free, out of that hospital with his family.

At this point, we had another family situation brewing at the same time. My brother Rob had two daughters at the time. Marissa, who was four years old, and Angelina who was ten months old. Angelina was born with a connective tissue disorder, called Marfans disease.

At the time, Angelina was on the cardiac floor at CHOP, recovering from one of her many surgeries in such a short time.

The whole family was at CHOP for Christmas Eve, traveling floor to floor to spend time with Angelina, as well as Matt. I said to my brother Rob, "I am going to be here for the duration of this round; why don't you go home and spend Christmas Eve with Marissa. I'll go check on Angelina throughout the night." As the night drew to dusk, people were leaving the hospital, nurses were changing shifts, and the whole floor started feeling eerie. Matt was asleep at the time, so I ventured to the sixth floor to visit Angelina, My heart just broke seeing this precious little girl struggling after her intense heart surgery. I said to myself, I can't believe we have two family members in hospital at the same time!

As I went back to Matt's room, I noticed an Elf dressed in a green outfit, leaving Matt's room. Sure enough, the elf left a gift on the foot of Matt's bed. I thought that gesture was pretty amazing. Christmas still lives in the hearts of everyone at CHOP.

As the sun started to rise Christmas Day, Matt was awake. "Mom come over here. Get over here, right now!" He said, "Merry Christmas Mom, I love you." He grabbed me and held on as tight as he could, I just did not want to ever let go. I knew rounds were going to start at 9:00 a.m. and I needed coffee. I asked Matt if he wanted a donut, Of course he wanted a jelly donut.

As I ventured to the cafeteria, I find out that the cafeteria was closed. Well, looks like I'm going to WaWa. I walked four blocks to get WaWa. It was a cold and desolate journey. There were no cars in the street, or a sole to be found. As I reached my destination, the convenient store was closed! I could not believe this was happening, no coffee or donut for us today. As headed back to the hospital, in utter disappointment, this Christmas day is not starting off to a good start.

As I entered the room, Dave and the boys were already here. There were gifts all over the room, ready to be unwrapped by all. The boys waited to get to the hospital to open up their gifts from Santa. The boys stayed all day with Matt. This round was the longest round by far; We were finally discharged by New Year's Day.

After a clean MRI and spinal tap, plans for the final round were underway...

Finally, we are in the final round of chemotherapy. How are we all going to get through this final round together? We have experienced hallucinations, a life-threatening infection, severe weight loss, and those horrific chemotherapy drugs.... Where are we going to get the strength to get through the last round?

As we gear up for round five, the chief of oncology enters the room to talk to us. He said, "I never in my thirty years of practicing Oncology, have I seen such a strong mother, you have been a cheerleader for Matt, you have gotten him this far, and you will make it to the finish line."

We all were feeling defeated at this point. Matt was starting to look like a skeleton.

I tried not to think if Matt did not pull through with final round.

This was the middle of January, and the temperature in Philadelphia had started to drop. It was a little too cold to take a walk outside with those blustery winds hitting me in the face.

When we started the first round, I walked a lot to clear my head. I needed to get out of the hospital for about 45 minutes each day. Exercise was always therapy for me. At a young age of fifteen, I would ride my bike to the gym for exercise. The endorphin release has been a physical and emotional high for me. Exercise got me through stressful times in my dysfunctional childhood.

Matt would say, "Hey, Mom aren't you going to walk today?" "I'm getting tired of looking at you."

Matt was living on vanilla ice cream, Oreo cookies, and Reece's "BIG CUPS". Whatever he wanted to eat and if he was enjoying it, nothing else mattered. Of course, the threat of the NG tube was always in the back of my mind. The suggestion of Marinol, (THC) in a pill form would be added to his treatment plan. An increase in appetite and decrease in nausea was the ultimate goal. We thought this would be a great idea. At this point in treatment, the chemo was wearing on his body. The MRI and spinal tap had shown no areas of cancer cells. I thought to myself, why do we need to go ahead with the fifth round?"

It was three days and counting until Matt and Tommy's fourteenth birthday. I know we had to get him home to celebrate his birthday with his twin brother. Matt did say to me, Mom, so are you going to get me out of this hospital?" I replied, Oh, yes Matt, I will get you out of here!"

After I promised reassurance to Matt's request, The Physician on call that weekend enters the room and tells us that Matt cannot be discharge, due to his weight. I said to the physician, "Can you please step outside of the room so we can talk?" I tried to remain calm, but my frustration got the best of me. I said to the doctor, "You are going to get your pen and sign those discharge papers right now!" Her rebuttal, "Mrs. Renk we cannot discharge you son, he is eighty-nine pounds!" I continued my argument with her. "We are getting out of this hospital today. So, please sign the discharge papers, and I will fatten him up at home." She continued her ridiculous explanation of why he needs to stay. "We need to put the NG tube in on Monday morning." As we know in previous conversations regarding the NG tube, that was never going to happen on my watch. She agreed to sign the discharge papers. I walked back in to Matt's room, "Who's your Mama?" He responded, "yes, you got me out of here!" he was so ecstatic. "Mom your awesome, I just knew you could do it!" He had his bags packed within minutes, waiting at the door. I wanted to prove to Matt that anything is possible with a little perseverance.

As we were driving home from chemo, Matt calls his father and told him that, "Mom got me out of the hospital three days before I was supposed to leave, and Dad, we are on I-95 driving home." Dave's reply on speaker, "Your mom never ceases to amaze me!"

The key to this whole round was to have the boys together for their birthday!

In my over-the-top grand celebration, we had all friends and family over the house to celebrate the boys' birthday and Matt's victory of five grueling rounds of chemotherapy!

The day was spectacular to see everyone over celebrating this triumphant accomplishment.

Two weeks have past, and Matt lets us know that he is ready to go back to school.

He has missed six months of school.

Matt was adamant about his return to school, but of course, I felt that we needed to wait just a little longer. Matt wanted me to call the principal to let him know that he was ready to return to school. Tommy was apprehensive about the decision. Tommy said, "I don't think Matt is ready to go back yet, he is just too skinny." Tommy's reservations were real; he did not want attention drawn to his brothers' appearance. Matt's appearance internalized for Tommy.

Matt entered Holicong Middle school two weeks after his final round of chemo. He marched through the hallways weighing 89 pounds, not a stich of hair on his head. Tommy observed the merriment for all of Matt's peers. Tommy said, Mom, it was quite amazing the Welcome back which Matt received. One of the noteworthy comments, "Matt, you are truly our hero!"

The dynamic duo returned from school that afternoon with pure joy. Recollecting the last time this duo was together was when Matt threw up on the bus. Tommy was overjoyed to have his twin brother back!

Matt worked diligently at the kitchen table catching up on his assignments. He stated with determination, "Mom I have to catch up to eight grade!"

As the months moved forward, June was approaching for the three-month check at the hospital. Matt was back on the golf course helping his dad, and knew it was time to go back to CHOP for his MRI and spinal tap. We are now facing the one-year mark since Matt was diagnosed.

Again, MRI and spinal tap showed no signs of cancer cells! We all were pretty excited with the news!

We as a family were getting our lives back. I went back to work with the Surgeons. Tommy was playing football, getting ready for tryouts for the High school team. Andrew playing baseball, and Matt was playing golf, as well. Matt and I went back to our Monday afternoon ritual playing golf. Matt's strength was not totally back, so we played only four holes. With sheer determination on Matt's part, he wanted to try out for the golf team. I thought to myself, How in God's name is that going to happen?

Later that night, after our round of golf, Tommy was sitting on the porch with a sad look on his face. Matt said, "Tommy why are you not a football practice today?" Tommy replied, "I quit the football team today." Matt leaps out of the chair, and screams at the top of his lungs at Tommy.

"Tom, you are a jackass! You spent all that time practicing, and now you decide to quit? I know I am will not make the golf team, but I am sure going to try." The bantering back and forth from the boys was priceless. This captivating moment of why I was chosen to be a mother of twins was apparent.

A year later....

Matt's "Make a wish" was granted. His wish was not the average wish from a child. He wanted a John Deer gator cart. The usual wish from a child with a terminal illness may meet a famous superstar, or a family vacation. Matt was all about moving on with his life, and cancer was way behind him now.

We had family and friends over to witness this joyous event. Matt was ecstatic when the "Make A Wish team showed upon our driveway!

We are now in remission for fourteen months, Matt looks awesome, gaining weight, and getting his strength back. He returned from school that Friday afternoon, knowing he needed to go to his MRI that night at CHOP. He said, "Mom, I really do not want to go back to the hospital again, I'm fine, no need to worry." I tried to distract him by suggesting, "What movie are you going to watch in the MRI? He was pissed! He had no response. I packed Transformers, and Iron Man for him.

As we pulled into the parking garage, Matt said, "I'm hungry, let's go to the cafeteria and eat before I have to go into that stupid ass machine." As we sat across from each other, I just stared at him in amazement of what this young man has been through, and his strength got me through of this entire catastophe.

The MRI was scheduled for 7:00 p.m., and we were delayed because the nurses could not find a vein on either of Matt's arms. The scars on his arms were not of a fourteen-year-old. As I tried to occupy myself in the reception area, I looked at my phone and discover that Matt had been in the MRI for over 3.5 hours. This has been the longest he has ever been in an MRI. Dave called several times, "Is he out yet?" After a four-hour MRI, he comes out of the MRI with his eyes red and huge circles around his eyes. The first word he said, "Mom, are you okay?" I responded, "The question is, are you okay?" He said, "Let's get the hell out of here." He grabbed his John Deer hat and ran for the elevator. There was something about that night that did not seem right to me. The whole weekend I was checking my phone to see if the Oncologist had left a message. By Sunday night, I felt no news was good news. Our appointment with the oncologist was for the following Tuesday morning.

As we sat in the clinic waiting to be called back, I noticed Matt's oncologist walk right by us.

She had a very somber look on her face, but I did not take her emotion to heart.

When the doctor entered the room, she asked me, "Did you come by yourself today?" I replied, "Yes, I did, why do you ask?" She said, "I wanted to call you over the weekend, but need to speak to you in person." In a straight, emotionless expression, she said, "THE TUMOR IS BACK ON THE FRONTAL LOBE OF MATT'S BRAIN AND THREE SPOTS ON HIS SPINE." My entire body was frozen. She started to ramble about this and that. I said, "Please don't say another word, I cannot comprehend anything that is coming out of your mouth right now!!!!" I got up walked over to the wall and pinched it as hard as I could. I screamed, "I can't believe its back, I can't believe its back!" I walked over to Matt and I said, "Are you okay?"

He responded, "You're not okay Mom, I will be fine." I said to the oncologist, "I got to get the hell out of here, and go home, I can't handle what you just told me." "I really don't know how I am going to drive home now." I told her as soon as we get home, we will have a conference call with Dave, after I calm down a little." All she said to me, "I am sorry, Matt was doing so well."

My heart was racing out of my chest, sick to my stomach, and now I will have to drive home.

How am I going to tell Dave???? Matt grabbed me and hugged me so hard! "Mom, you need to calm down." The doctor instructed me to sit for a while before I drove home. I said, "I have to get the hell out of here!

As I was driving on I-95, Dave was calling and texting me. I just could not tell him over the phone. Matt was sitting next to me with his ear buds listening to music.

I called my sister, and she did not answer my call. I did not want to bother my brother, because he was in the early stages of grief, with the loss of his daughter Angelina. She passed on Memorial Day weekend of May 2010. I proceeded to call my brother, and he answered right away. I said, "Rob, you got to help me get home."

He replied, "What's the matter? Are you okay?"

I blurred it out, "THE TUMOR IS BACK."

He said, "Are you frickin' kidding me? Just come over my house and calm down!"

I said, "I got to get home and tell Dave." Rob insisted that I was in no condition to drive back to Bucks County. I said, "Just keep me on the phone until I get to 413." When I felt more confident in my mental status, I told Rob, "Thanks for getting me home, I call you over the weekend." I know I needed to call my sister to let her know of this horrible news. I called my sister when I got to 413. I told her the news, and instantly she burst into tears. She said, "I got to get out of my office, just get home safe. Jack, I just have no words!"

In the meantime, Matt was sitting next to me and getting frustrated with me that I am not answering Dave's calls, which were coming through the bluetooth every ten minutes. Matt said, "Mom, why are you not answering Dad's calls?" I said, I'll talk to him when we get home."

As we pulled into the driveway, my stomach was in knots. Dave was in the kitchen pacing back and forth. Dave immediately said, "Why weren't you answering your phone. What happened?"

I blurred out, "THE TUMOR IS BACK." His face turned white. He replied, "There is no way in hell that the tumor is back!" Matt followed slowly behind me. Dave approached Matt and both hugged each other and cried their eyes out.

Matt said to his father, "Dad, I do not want to die." Dave and I just starred at each other, and words did not come out of our mouths.

I told Dave after several unsettled moments later, "The oncologist will be calling later this afternoon to review Matt's MRI results." I just could not comprehend anything she was telling us earlier in her office. Matt left the room to go lay down on the couch. Dave said, "I need to go on the course and try to digest what you just told me." I was looking out of the kitchen window in shock. Later, I walked out of the house to sit by the pool to gather my thought of how was I going to tell Tommy and Andrew. I knew both boys were coming home from school shortly, and I did not have much time.

As I recalled from our last conversation with the chief of Oncology, prior to Matt's final day of chemotherapy. I said, "Doc, what happens if the tumor comes back?" He stated, "We could do a clinical trial, but these tumors come back with a vengeance." Of course, he was absolutely correct.

My phone rang later that afternoon, and it was Matt's oncologist on the phone. Dave and I were sitting together at the kitchen table waiting for her call. She first apologized that she had to give us this horrible news. She said, "Matt has an inoperable brain tumor that is located in his frontal lobe (hypothalamus). Also, there are three spots on his spine that have cancer cells. We cannot operate again, nor do radiation. We can only participate in a clinical trial."

We both had some many questions to ask: How did this happen? We had five clean MRIs since surgery. How did the tumor come back? She replied, "Cancer cells are sometimes hidden behind normal cells."

As we ended the call, Dave and I both grabbed each other and cried our eyes out. The embrace which we both shared was so powerful that we just did not want to let go, nor of our son Matthew.

I never thought telling my story would be so difficult to express, let alone write about the history in great detail.

Andrew and Tommy came into the kitchen laughing and punching each other. Both stopped in their tracks, "What's wrong with the two of you?"

I said, "Guys come out to the porch, we have to talk to the both of you."

As we tried to gather the right words to tell the boys, my heart was broken to tell them the news...

Andrew said, "Oh, that sucks that the tumor came back." His innocent little face was enough to put anyone in a tailspin. All four of us were sitting there waiting for someone else to speak.

Matt came walking out to the porch, with attitude in full force. "What is wrong with all of you?" The intensity of that day was starting to come to fruition. Tommy was in shock, with a confused look on his face. Andrew was so young at the time he just didn't know how to react. We all react to stress in different ways. Matt and Tommy had that connection; Twin bonding, and their gift of telepathy. Both boys just looked at each other and started jumping on the couch and wrestling. Andrew was kind of by the wayside. He never seemed to want to get interconnected with that twin bonding. He just had the presence of mind at such a young age, that his brothers' relationship was a very unique relationship. I wanted all three boys to bond together. I said," Let me get some pictures of all of you." I just was starting taking pictures incisively. We needed to hold on to this moment, I thought to myself.

The next day, I wanted to play golf and I knew this would be the last time I was ever going to play golf with Matt. In a few days we would have to start treatment. I approached Matt and Tommy and I said,

"Let's play golf," Tommy said, "Can I caddie for you and Matt?" Tommy knew of the golf relationship that his brother and I shared, and he just wanted to be a part of this final round. Also, he did not want to be out of Matt's sight for even two minutes. Matt and Tommy were just so much fun. I thought this might be the last time I will spend time with my twins. I didn't want to think about the outcome the entire round. As we headed on the 18th green, I tried to bury my emotions, but the tears started to roll down my cheeks. Tommy said, "Mom, are you okay?"

I replied, "I'm okay, just sweating too much, it's hot out here."

As the weekend approached us, Dave thought we should have our families over to see Matt t before he started chemo. I thought to have everyone over was too much for me right now! Dave insisted that Matt needs everybody. No one knew what to say to Matt. Nobody knew how to react. They were just going through the motions and I think everybody knew, too, that this could be the last of Matt. I was completely numb all weekend. The agony of getting kicked in the stomach all over again.

As the evening grew to a close, I noticed that Dave and Matt were missing. I looked in the garage, and saw the Dave's cart was gone. Dave and Matt were taking a cart ride around the golf course. I knew what Dave was thinking. This was going to be Matt's last cart ride.

I just wanted everyone to go home. I had enough for today.

Dave came back with his eyes were bloodshot from crying. Matt seemed a little startled. Dave said to me, "Matt's really scared." Our minds were focused on Matt. Dave said, "I just can't believe this is happening to us again." We're going down this road again and knowing what the road was prior to this re-diagnosis."

The next day we had to pack up the car and head to the hospital. This will be a full week of chemotherapy. My brother called me and asked, "How are you?" I said, "Well, not good." He said, "I'm going to come with you. I'm going to come with you and help you unpack." We're in the garage at the hospital, and my brother was unpacking the car and he sees a case of water in the trunk. "Wow, you have some stuff in this trunk." I said, "This is my summer vacation, a week at CHOP ... I'm spending a week here." He thought that was pretty ironic. I said, "Rob, I am getting kind of immune to what is ahead of me."

My brother, and I had a great bonding that day. He's helping me unpack and I said to my brother, "I can't do this by myself." We were admitted into the room; Rob was running up and down the steps bringing all the cargo from the car. I said, "We'll probably get the chemo started within a few hours." We were just sitting around waiting for the start of chemo. Matt was playing with his phone with my brother and downloading movies. This clinical trial did not have the intensity as opposed to the last five rounds. The first couple of drugs that were administered did not get him sick. My brother and I were sitting there waiting for the vomiting to start. Matt said, "Uncle Rob, can you get me pizza?" I never saw my brother run as fast as he did. He returns with pizza and a milkshake. Matt scarfed the pizza down within a few minutes. I believe the combination of the Marinol and Zofran on board helped with his appetite and nausea. He had the cutest smile on his face, resting peacefully after his stomach was full. Rob left shortly after Matt feel asleep. I was forever grateful to have my brother there for emotional support. Later that night I texted my brother to tell him that Matt kept the pizza down.

In the middle of the week, we find out that My Uncle Danny passed away from lung cancer. He too suffered from this insidious disease. I was beside myself that I was not able to attend his funeral. He was an inspiration and a true man that I admired deeply. Matt knew I was upset that I could not attend. He insisted that I should go, but I was torn to leave Matt alone. Also, I did not want everyone to ask me how Matt was doing.

Friday morning comes and Matt pops out of bed. He said in his raspy voice, "Mom we are getting the hell out of here today!" We're just sitting in his room waiting and waiting for glucose drip. This was like waiting for paint to dry. The nurses would come to check his vitals. Matt would ask, "When the hell am I getting out of here? I got to get the hell out of here." He had his backpack by the door. He said, "Mom, come on get your stuff packed. Little did he know we had some time before he was going to be discharged. He was a great solider, his attitude was as follows; I want to take this crap off and get the hell out of here. I did my duty. I fought the fight and I'm out of here.

The nurses responded to Matt's demands, "We're going to get out later today," and Matt would look at me and say, "Come on, Mom. Are you going to accept that now?" I said, "The sugar water has got to go through you. We got to go through those two bags." He said, in a very disappointed manner, "Can you tell the nurse to get the Xbox, so I can kick your ass in golf?" We played every game you can imagine doing our hospital stays. We were very entertained with many episodes of *Seinfeld*. At the time, Tiger Woods virtual golf was the game we played. We were having a blast yelling and screaming at each other. Mind you we just did five straight days of chemotherapy and we're at the last day and this kid was having a blast. We caused such a ruckus in the hospital that five nurses came in and said, "What's going on here?" Matt said, "I'm kicking my mom's ass in golf." They were belly laughing. They thought that was so funny that this kid is just having a great time with his mom. That night I don't think we were discharged till eight o'clock that night. We packed up the stuff and we schlepped down to the parking garage.

Once we got on. I-95, Matt called his Dad, saying, "I'm coming home! You guys better be ready. We're on 95." I drove fast that night because I wanted to get home. "Mom, you better slow down,"

"I just want to get home, Matt." We walked into the door, Tommy standing and waiting for Matt with that twin embrace again.

Andrew was coming back from baseball drops his baseball bag. "Oh, there's my bubby."

The next day we're all just hanging out by the pool. Matt was pretty tired, but I brought him out by the pool to be with his brothers. At his particular moment in time, I knew this was the last picture of all three of my boys together.

Monday morning came around; we had to get some blood work done. Dave came with me to the CHOP satellite office in Chalfont, Pennsylvania. Dave needed to help Matt out of the truck because Matt was very weak, and was having trouble walking on his own. When returned home, Matt took a nap for several hours. I was checking on him constantly. This day remains vivid in my mind. This traumatic scene was one of the most intricate parts of my PTSD. Matt came staggering out of the family room and heads out to the outside porch. He makes it to the couch, and plops down. Tommy was directly cattycorner to him on the opposing chair. Dave was playing with the radio station; Andrew was with me in the kitchen. I went to pour a glass of wine and I took the one sip and walked out at the porch. As my eyes looked up, I saw Matt's body was hallucinating. He was shaking out of control and I let out the loudest scream. I said, "What the hell is happening?" He couldn't stop shaking and I went over and I grabbed him.

"Matt, are you okay?" I quickly got on the phone and called the oncologist. The oncologist on call told me to call 911. My hands were shaking to even dial the phone.

He was just shaking out of control.

Within three minutes, Lingohoken Fire Company was at my house and the firemen came in the back door with a gurney. I remember these two big guys came in with fire chief. Andrew was so concerned that the fire company wouldn't find our house because our house sat far back. Andrew got on his bike to the end of the driveway to wait for the firemen. He said, to fire chief, "You got to help my brother." The fire chief said, "Your son was at the front of the driveway to make sure we could get to the house." The two firemen placed Matt on the gurney, and at that point I knew Matt was never coming home. Tommy's face was completely white. Andrew was crying excessively. Dave and I were completely numb. I called one of my girlfriends to stay with Andrew and Tommy because Dave had to come with me. The fire chief said, "Are you going to be coming with us?" and I said, "Yes, are we going to CHOP?" and he says, "No. We have to go to Doylestown Hospital," His reply, he further stated, "Mrs. Renk, you did the right thing by calling us because there's no way that you would have been able to handle this getting him to CHOP," and he said, "We'll get him to Doylestown and then we'll get him transported down to CHOP."

I got in the ambulance, Dave followed us in his truck and we were brought to Doylestown Hospital. Matt was having the shakes excessively, and he started to vomit in the ambulance. After we were admitted to the emergency room at Doylestown Hospital, several hours later were then transported to CHOP. I said to the ambulance driver, "Can you drive little faster?" "My son is struggling back there!" My anxiety and stress took the best of me again! We arrive to CHOP at midnight.

We are in the emergency room at CHOP, waiting for a doctor to access Matt's situation. The hallucinations, vomiting, and the diarrhea were getting uncontrollable. It's just all over the place. I'm calling for nurses. "You got to help me! You got to help me!" Matt was holding on to me, and shaking like a leaf. I gave up trying to clean up the bed. I just held on to him so he would not hallucinate and fall. This night turned into one of those long nights. After many blood tests, the physician came in and confrimed that Matt had pneumonia.

The last night at home, Matt was up all night coughing and spitting up blood. I believe that was the correlation to the Pneumonia. I said to the attending physician, "My son has pneumonia and no immune system, that does not sound too good?" She said, He is going to be on a strong antibiotic for a while. "We're going to bring him up to ICU in about an hour, just waiting for a bed to open. She left the room quickly because her other four beepers were going off. In the meantime, I can't keep my eyes open.

One of the interns taps me on the shoulder, "Mrs. Renk, we are bringing your son to critical ICU, just follow the team."

This unit was the most intense ICU that one could imagine. The words that I can describe are a warzone. As Matt was wheeled up to the critical ICU, I was not prepared for this scene. The doors open to the unit, and the bombs started going off in my mind. I started to feel like a solider entering Afghanistan. The only words to describe this scene was a warzone. As we walked through the doors the intensity was starting to implode. The unit may have twenty-five glass-partitioned rooms. My heart started beating out of my chest as I saw Doctors and nurses running through the barracks to attend to a child who had just coded. The blue light was alarming the entire unit. Each room had many people attending to each child in each room or (barracks). That was my poignant interpretation. I thought I was going to have a nervous breakdown. What I just went through in the past twelve hours and now I just entered Afghanistan. Walking in this unit the only way I could describe was crawling on my hands and knees under the barbwire fence, waiting for the enemy to attack. As I was crawling to the room the barbwire was cutting me in the back, as I witness the expressions on the parents faces. The intensity on these parents' faces was enough for me to understand their anguish and despair. Deep down inside I was scared for the future of my son. As walked around the barracks that day to fetch some water, I had difficulties putting on foot in front of another because of the extreme exhaustion and anxiety. The sights and sounds of the unit made the oncology floor feel like the Four Seasons Hotel. I thought to myself how am I going to get through this nightmare. As I entered the sliding glass door of Matt's Platoon, there were 6 people setting him up to a multitude of equipment and monitors. That evening the nurse stood by Matt's bedside taking his vital signs and writing notes all night. She would occasionally ask if I needed anything. I said, in a cathartic tone, "A difference diagnosis would be perfect?"

The next morning, the entourage of doctors came to Matt's bedside. The doctors asked if I would step outside for rounds. I did not know why the conversation had to be outside?

One of the physicians said, "We have to put Matt on oxygen because he's having trouble breathing." The thought of oxygen led to my PTSD triggers of anxiety. Oxygen means that my son's lungs are starting to fail.

At this point I haven't eaten in three days. I went down to the cafeteria because I needed to get out of the war zone for a little bit. I remember walking down the hallway and so much was going through my mind of what happened. I've been here back and forth for two years. I've been walking down these hallways for years and I remember getting on the elevator and I didn't know where I was going. The gentleman on the elevator said, "What floor?" I said, "I don't know where I'm going/." I was delusional from lack of sleep, stress, and anxiety. I eventually got downstairs and headed to the cafeteria. I needed to eat something because I'm going to pass out.

I remember being down in that cafeteria the night of the last MRI. Matt and I were down there and he ate like a wolf that day. He said, "Mom, this cafeteria is great." I remember us laughing before the MRI. all of these emotions, all these flashbacks were going through my mind. I sat down and try to eat and the nausea started to set in. I went back upstairs to Matt's room and oxygen facemask was on his face. I turned to the left and there's was huge stand full of antibiotics that was pumped into him constantly. There must have been five to seven different medications constantly being pumped into him. Matt. "Are you okay?" and "Do you need anything?"

"No, Mom. I'm okay. Mom, just sit next to me." I sat next to him and all of a sudden, I start getting diarrhea. I raced to the bathroom; all of the stress started to release out of me all at once. I was crying in the bathroom trying to hold back the tears. He said, in a muffled voice, "Mom, are you all right?" I said, "Matt, I'm fine." "Okay, Mom" was his reply.

Matt knew that I starting to fall apart mentally and physically.

I received a phone call from Dr. Mellen later that afternoon.

He knew that Matt was sick but was not sure of why he called me. I always trusted him; he saved my life a few times. Dr. Mellen said, "Jackie, you got to sleep. You got to sleep. I'm going to prescribe you some Xanax to relax you just a bit. You can't go on like this anymore. You have to be making decisions and you have to think clearly," and I said, "How do I sleep in a warzone?" He said, "Jackie, you are the most remarkable woman. You have been a patient of mine for a long time, and I know the struggles that you have been through. I will say to you that you gave Matt the best fifteen years and you take that and you cherish it. You are a remarkable mother, and I want you to try to take care of yourself. If you need me, I'm here."

I needed to hear his words of wisdom. I'm just doing what I have to do as a mom. I'm not remarkable. I worked hard to be strong. I was outside of Matt's room sitting in the lobby overlooking the Abramson Center. Matt and I watched that building progress in the two years during treatment. We never got that opportunity of taking advantage of Proton therapy. The tumor could not be targeted, and the spots on his spine were not tangible. I sat there in a daze trying to collect my thoughts. I knew that Dave was coming later on that day. The infectious disease Drs. would come in every day and tell us about the different antibiotics that they were going to give him. I said, "Okay, I'm not a rocket scientist, but you keep giving him all these antibiotics and he doesn't have an immune system. So, how are these going to work?" The team would reply, "We're doing our best. It's going to take time to work."

Dave came in that afternoon without the boys. We were sitting on the bench discussing what the infectious disease doctors came in to discuss. Matt would take the mask off to speak to us. This mask was very uncomfortable for him to sleep and speak. I was standing by Matt's bed, trying to understand what he was trying to tell me. He was asking for his dad to come to his bedside as well. This was the most amazing compelling, and heartbreaking request that I ever heard from anyone, especially from our son. He said, "Dad, come over here. Come over to my bed." Dave walked over and we're both standing there in front of Matt. He takes the facemask off and said to Dave, "Dad, please take great care of mom because I'm going to be okay."

Dave's face ... while he hesitated for a minute and said to Matt, "Don't worry. I'll take care of Mom. Everything will be okay." After that startling revelation, Matt knew that his time here was coming to a close. He wanted to make sure that his mom was going to be okay before he left this world!

At this moment we knew he had given up his fight. For as strong as this kid was for over two years, the fight was over. In Matt's mind, I can't do this anymore. I'm struggling here. I'm drowning Mom....

Dave and I just stared at each other; We didn't have much to say.

I did take the Xanax that night.

There was no place to sleep. I set up camp on a bench every night. I slept on a bench in Matt's Barracks.

Dave went home ten o'clock that evening. I just get a few hours of sleep. I was nervous to take the Xanax because I didn't know how I was going to react towards this medication. I still needed to be alert.

As I rested my head on the bench, staring at the ceiling, reflecting on the day and the days prior. Why is this happening? I remember it was 1:30 in the morning when I hear that great little voice, "Mom, come here. Come over here. Are you okay?" I said, "Matt, I'm fine." I remember getting up and in that little stupor of sedation. I was tripping over stuff and falling trying to get there as fast as I can. The nurse didn't leave for a second constantly take Matt's vitals.

He wanted me to be next to him!

I was still changing him because he had… a diaper on again; The antibiotics were giving him violent diarrhea. I lay right next to him that night. He wanted me every minute of each day.

The next night I woke up in a Xanax stupor, due to all the commotion going on in the barracks. A child coded. The alarms went off. I woke up out of my stupor, I would call it because I never felt like I ever slept. I felt like I took a nap at CHOP for two years. I get up off my bench and mind you there's no doors. There's just a sliding-clear-glass door. Every patient needs to be monitored in critical ICU. I look up and see the blue alarms going off. So obviously, a bomb was just dropped. A huge M80 was just dropped in that room next to us. That's what I describe a bomb was dropped. I got up to see the damage in the barracks. I look over and there's a mom crunched down in the hallway on the floor with her head in her hands. Her son just passed. She's hysterical crying and my heart broke for her. I walk out of the room and I just wanted to console her. She was there by herself and she was leaned up against the wall. I went over to her. I said, "I'm so sorry." Her eyes were swollen shut, she gazed up at me and said, "I just lost my son." She was just hit by a bullet and I was there put that tourniquet on to stop the bleeding. She just got shot, and I needed to be the brave solider for the platoon. I just knew that she was a mom that was in excruciating pain. Her heart was just blown away. I stayed with her for a little bit longer that night. She said, "Go back and be with your son."

The unit was just mayhem.

I sat on the edge of Matt's bed staring into space. I knew I was not going to sleep that night.

The next morning, I went down to go get coffee, two cups of strong coffee. On my way back to the room, A picture of a flower was placed on the outside of the boys' room that passed the night before.

The flower symbolizes that a child just passed. The sense of death became surreal. Walking by that little boy's room left me feeling freezing cold and stricken with grief.

No mother ever wants to share with another mother, the death of a child. You never ever want to feel those crippling emotions with any mother. I was going through a series of emotions myself. Where am I? We are knocking on heaven's door. Look where we are?

Later that afternoon, Dave came to the hospital, "You got to go home because the boys are really missing you. You got to go home today." We did switch. We called in the changing of guards. He met me downstairs. I got in the car and he went back upstairs and I drove back home, I went back home and I just was in awe and at this particular point. There was another tragedy in my family. I lost my uncle to lung cancer during this time of Matt being diagnosed before the first round of chemo, July 9 of 2010, I lost my godfather and I couldn't go to the funeral because I was at CHOP. Matt did say, "Why don't you go to Uncle Danny's funeral?" Still today, I am heartbroken that I could not attend his funeral. My uncle was a legend of his time. He was the most caring, warm man I've ever met. He always took care of me when I was a young girl. He was there for me when the boys were born, giving me the positive inspiration. His spirituality was precedent like no one else. He went to church every day and taught catechism.

Losing my godfather was tragedy number two in my family within two months losing my niece, Angelina.

I stayed with the boys for two nights. Andrew and Tommy were concerned with Matt's condition. They both were full of questions, and I had no answers.

I went back to the hospital that Sunday afternoon. Dave and I were alone for a while, before the entourage of family members arrived: my sister-in-law- Lori, my sister-Joanne, and my brother-in-law- Paul. The doctor came and told to us that they were going to put Matt on the ventilator. When Dave heard that news, he got this huge cramp on the side that he couldn't even move. He became paralyzed for a while. He was in distress from the horrifying news. I never have seen Dave cry so much in the twenty-five years of marriage. He was inconsolable. I said to our family, as we sat in the lobby trying to console Dave. I said, "Matt's going to leave this world just the way he came in on a ventilator." No one said too much after my outburst. We all wanted to be with Matt before he was intubated.

Matt had to be sedated before he was intubated. I knew this was the last time I'm going to ever hear my son speak again. I grabbed him and I said, "Matt, I love you." "No, Mom. I love you more." We always went back and forth, nope, I love you more, nope I love you more and that's where we would banter back and forth. The nurses said, "you got to leave now because we got to get ready. I said, "No, I'm staying with him. No, I'm not ready to leave yet." My sister, Theresa and Lori took my hand and escorted me out of the room.

After an hour or two the nurse called us back in the room. To see Matt on ventilator brought back his arrival in the NICU at Pennsylvania Hospital. My God, that was only 15 years ago. Dave took one look at Matt, and let out an outburst of tears. To watch your husband cry as much as he did that afternoon made my heart break even further.

The first night on the ventilator Dave said, "I want this night by myself with Matt."

I said, "Okay. Are you going to be okay here by yourself?" Dave reassured me that he would be fine. I went back home again and Andrew was cute as he could be.

"Mom, let's go to Mosquito Grill tonight for dinner, okay?" We went to Mosquito Grill because he loved wings. This was the last thing I wanted to do, but when I was given this gift to become a mother you lose yourself. It doesn't matter how I feel. It matters how my kids feel. My children gave me the strength each day. Andrew said, "Oh, are we going to get the real hot ones, Mom?" My stomach was in no condition for hot wings. I ate the hot wings, and then I remember I threw up in the bathroom within minutes. I needed to stay in the bathroom and regain my composure before I returned to the table. Andrew asked if he could sleep in my bed that night, because Dad was with Matt and he needed to be next to me.

Tommy was, at a friend's house that evening, and returned home after Andrew and I got home from dinner. We tried to keep him caddying at the golf course to keep his mind off Matt's condition, but it didn't work. At this point, Tommy kept calling me every day, of course, and a couple times a day. Is Matt getting better? Is Matt getting better? He still didn't understand the whole concept of what was going on.

Before I headed back to the hospital, I needed another blanket because I was getting really cold at the hospital. As I was standing impatiently in the long line at Marshalls. I was thinking to myself, *nobody knows what I'm going through.* Why is that lady laughing? Will I ever laugh again? Will I survive losing my son? I got to get out of here.

I headed back to the hospital, and the usual support team was present. Paul, Joanne, Rob and Theresa. Dave was a mirror image of my thoughts as I looked at him gazing over Matt's face bedside. He was talking to Matt about the golf course.

My brother was ecstatic to show me his new creation on his arm. "I have something to show you," He lifts up his shirt to show his amazing tattoo of his daughter Angelina in the arms of an angel on his shoulder. I said, "Holy, smokes that's big," We don't do anything in a small way. We do everything in a big way. The best artwork I've ever seen. Rob was trying to redirect my mind for a little.

Right before Matt went on the ventilator, the team wanted to give Matt his stem cells. As stated prior, we reserved his cells before he started the clinical trial. We had to go through Apheresis for a second time. When Matt got his cells, his lungs were flooded will the new stem cells. There was a distinct odor when he got his cells back. The preservative reminded me of tomato soup. I can't take the smell of tomato soup, even after several years later.

I was accepting the realization that it was just a matter of time when I was going to lose my son.

Monday, August 9, 2010, was the loneliest day of my life. I woke up that morning, the nurses would allow me to go to Matt's bedside to suction out Matt's mouth and I remember Matt was still trying to call for me. Calling for me, struggling. Waving his hands to get my attention. I said to the nurse, what's happening today? She said we just ordered some more blood for Matt. I remember there was some residual blood that just kept going back into the tube. The blood was recycling in the tube.

I said to her, "Stop giving him more blood! Save the blood for the kids that really need it. I need to know what is happening!"

She said, "I will let the attending physician know that you need to talk to him." She came into the room several hours later. "The doctor will talk to you around 3:00 today." That whole day I just sat in Matt's room next to him on pins and needles with anticipation. Dave was texting me, friends were texting me. I just shut my phone off. I couldn't handle it anymore. I couldn't talk to anybody anymore.

Finally, the doctor was ready for me. I went into his office and I said to him, "Just tell me right now, how much time does my son have?"

In an empathetic tone, he said, "Your son has twenty-four hours." I thought to myself, *was anybody going to tell me this?* I know they were trying to keep him comfortable. "We can keep Matt on the ventilator for a while."

I said, "Isn't this about quality of life? This is a shell of my son now." I walked out of his office.

As I walked down the hall of the ICU, backed down in my position, hands and knees, struggling through the barbed wire, and this time I was cut pretty bad. There is a trail of blood behind me. I got twenty-four hours left with my son's life. How does one digest a time limit with our son's life? As I crawled to Matt's room my knees started to buckle. The whole unit was spinning out of control in my thoughts.

I went across the street to Matt's favorite place, Potbelly where we went during his first round of chemo. I wanted to reflect and gather my plan for tomorrow. As I walked into the restaurant, I thought to myself, I couldn't believe this is happening. I quickly scurried out of the restaurant because the grief turned into a tailspin of uncontrollable crying. I sat on the steps and continued weeping for a good half of an hour. After I tried to gain my thoughts, I knew I had a lot of work to do in order for Andrew and Tommy to see Matt for the last time.

I dialed the phone to call Dave; my heart was in my throat. Why dear God? I said, "I just talked to the attending physician. We had a little come-to-Jesus meeting to find out what's going on; Matt has twenty-four hours." The phone was silent. The longest moment of silence. I waited as long as I could. I said, "I know you're still there?"

He finally responded, "Are you kidding me? Matt seemed to be doing okay yesterday. They were lowering the settings on the ventilator." I felt at that point, Dave and I were at two different wavelengths. He was seeing that there was hope and I knew there wasn't any hope.

I said, "I don't know what's worse, sitting here with Matt or having to tell Andrew and Tommy that Matt will be passing tomorrow? Dave knew the pain and anguish was ahead of him. Telling the boys was going to be one of the toughest moments in his life. Dave said, ugh, "We will be at the hospital around 1:00 tomorrow afternoon."

I went back up to Matt's room, after the trudge across the street from Potbelly's. I asked Matt's nurse," who's going to be Matt's nurse tomorrow? She said," I'm not sure" I said, "I need to make a request. I would like Melissa to be here as Matt's nurse tomorrow." She said, "I could make that happen." So, sure enough Melissa wasn't supposed to work that day and she did came in, per my request.

I thought Melissa was one of the best nurses during my experience in ICU, compassionate, warm and fuzzy. She really loved Matt, who didn't. That night I felt like I had to write. I started writing a note to Matt. I started writing him a letter about how I felt about this long journey we walked courageous together. We struggled, fought, and never gave up. I thought writing was therapeutic for me. I started to tell him how much I loved him, dropped the writing and ran over to his bed and cried until I could not cry anymore.

That night Dave called me to tell me that the boys were not doing well that evening. Tommy called me later that evening, the only phone call I took that night. He said, "Mom, Is Matt getting any better? "I have no words. I said, "we're doing everything we can to keep him comfortable." In the most upsetting tone, Tommy expressed that he knew he was going to lose his brother tomorrow. Then he said, "Mom, I'll see you tomorrow. I had to plan for of how am I going to do this. How am I going to let go tomorrow? How am I going to walk out of this hospital without my son? How am I going to go on with my life? So that night the lights were on in his room all night long.

August 10, 2010.

I started the process at 6:00 a.m. in the morning; Melissa came in for her shift. I said," thank God you're here because we have a lot of work to do today." She said, "Yeah I know, what's the plan, what do you want me to help you with?" I said we got to make Matt look really awsome for his brothers when they arrive this afternoon. I wanted the last time that the boys saw him the way he always looked, neat and put together.

I opened his suitcase to get out his golf shirt, tan shorts, and belt. I couldn't put his golf shirt on because of the ventilator. I cut the back portion of his shirt up the back and I put it on him I tucked it in and I put his belt on, he always wanted his shirt tucked in. He had a diaper on, I couldn't get the shorts on. I said to her, "Oh God how do I do this part? He has to have his shirt tucked in. I started to panic! She said, "Let's wait until they arrive, we have time. We took all the IVs out of his arms, and the only thing that was left was the ventilator.

In the meantime, I called my brother because he's been down this road, just three months ago, with his daughter Angelina. I said to Rob, "I need your help today, Matt's going to be passing today." He replied, "I'll be there in an hour." I had to have everybody in position for what was going to happen.

My brother arrives, I said, "You need to be here when Andrew comes to the room." He came in and he said goodbye to Matt, and then he walked out of the room. My sister in-law. Theresa works in the city, Rob and Theresa were the only family that I told that Matt was passing that day. Theresa came in, just kissed me and hugged me, kissed Matt and she walked out of the room. The two of them stayed patiently in the lobby.

Dave arrived with the boys. Matt was ready. We got the golf pants on, the belt was on, everything was tucked in because that's the way Matt looked every day of his short life. He looked great for what we had, to work with under these circumstances. Melissa said, "Wow, we really pulled that off together, didn't we?"

The doctor walked in, the same one I talked to yesterday, he said, in a somber tone, "At 3:45 today is when we're going to take Matt off the ventilator." The boys entered the room, shortly after the physician left. The boys have not seen Matt in two weeks. The last time they saw him he had been taken out of the house on a gurney. Andrew walked in and completely freaked out. He took one look at Matt and lost it, crying and screaming.

I said, "Someone get my brother!" Rob comes flying in and grabs Andrew just picks him up and takes him out of the room. Tommy had the saddest face I have ever seen in my life. The look of fear and despair. He went up to his twin brother's bedside and said in a broken voice, "I love you, buddy. You were the best brother ever, and I've missed you for a long time." Dave came to the bedside, He said to Matt, "You fought the toughest battle, now the fight is over. I can't see you in this pain any much longer. I'll take care of Mom. I love you Matty." Matt called for me one last time. "Mom." We all just sat there and spoke a few words. The pastor came in and was talking to us for a while, went over to Matt's bedside, and gave him his last rites.

The doctor came in with his team of residents because it was getting closer. I saw this team of residents coming in at the foot of Matt's bed all lined up. It must have been about four of them. I said to the doctor, "What the hell's this? What's this, you're going to watch my son die today?" I felt the anger coming on. "Everybody out, out, I want them out! This is our time." The team filed out after my explosion. Tommy and Dave were standing by the bedside.

I said, "I'm going to get in the bed (because he wants me to be right next to him." I got up next to him and the doctors came over and started lowering the settings on the ventilator. The monitors were turned off because they wanted it quiet. The tears were rolling down Tommy's face. Dave was shaking. I grabbed Matt really tight and I said, "You can stop fighting now, Matt, because I'm going to start fighting for you. I will fight for you to the day I die." I held on to him so tight. I put my hand on his heart and I felt his last heartbeat. The feeling in my hand went numb. The numbness was the emptiness of his heart. At 3:45 p.m. on August 10, 2010 we lost our son and brother to brain cancer.

After an hour lying next to Matt, Melissa came to the bedside, "Mrs. Renk we need to take Matt out of the room." I turned my head towards her. "How do I leave him here?" She said, "Come with me, let's go outside the room." She had tears exploding down her face. "You have to walk away now. This will be the hardest part for you to do! I have seen your passion, drive, and determination to carry on. Just yesterday when you wanted to donate Matt's heart to a child on the Cardiac floor. You are by far the most unselfish person I have ever meet. When a parent loses a child, the last thing on their mind is thinking about another soul."

As we gathered up Matt's belongings from his room, we walked down the hallway to get Andrew from Rob and Theresa. I knew I just had to keep walking. As we approached I95 on the way back to Bucks County, I looked in the back seat and saw Andrew and Tommy staring out the car window. The numbness was staring to come into effect that Matt was missing...

On August 11,2010, I woke up a little later that morning, and stepped my feet on the hardwood floor. I said to myself. Did I have a nightmare last night, or did this really happen yesterday? A parent worst nightmare is now my reality for the rest of my life.

As we started to prepare for the funeral, of course, my phone was blowing up with text messages and phone calls with loved ones sending their condolences. All four of us sat at the funeral home for over four hours planning Matt's service. We were trying to plan where we could have the service. All of a sudden, the principal from Matt's school called to send his condolences to the family. He asked, "What can he do to help us out?" I replied, "Can we have the service in the auditorium at Holicong Middle School? "We knew there would be a lot of people from the community that would be attending. The funeral home could not hold a large capacity of people. The principal was accommodating to our request.

After a week of planning, we had the service in the auditorium at the school. We had many photos throughout the school displaying our family memories. The school did an excellent job celebrating Matt's life. Every teacher, counselor, and student that ever meet Matt attended the funeral. With the addition of family and friends, we had well over two thousand people at the service. Our family friends, Kelly, Emily, and Katie sang the most beautiful tribute to Matt. The funeral was emotionally exhausting, nonetheless.

Later that afternoon at five o'clock, we planned to go over to the first hole at Lookaway, to spread Matt's ashes. We only had close family members to attend the most sacred tribute. The course was always closed on Mondays, and every Monday afternoon at five o'clock Matt and I played golf. We all gathered at the first tee box, the pastor said a few words about Matt. Tommy and I gathered the bag of ashes and proceeded down the first fairway, with his brothers' ashes trailing behind us. As the ashes fell to the ground, we both stopped and grabbed each other with the most extraordinary embrace. I waited until Tommy wanted to let go...

Grief... How does one Survive?

For the first couple of weeks after my son's death, My PTSD started to ignite. The flashbacks started to overtake my everyday life. I woke up every night in a complete sweat, trembling and shaking and feeling the presence of Matt standing at my bedside. My mind was going in many directions: Brain surgery, radiation, chemotherapy, and the birth of the twins. Again, I kept replaying in my mind, why did this happen? There must be a reason why this happened, I don't know right now. I'm going through this gut-wrenching pain and the pain was starting to cripple me. I describe grief as a crippling mechanism, wearing a heavy trench coat that you wear each day. The pain carries you were ever you go, and becomes a part of your everyday life. How do I go on with my life with the loss of my son? Others have tried to console me with their experiences. "I lost my grandmother, or I lost my dog last year, I know how you feel." No one knows the pain of WALKING IN THESE PAINFUL SHOES.

I knew I had to put one foot in front of the other and get back to work. I had to regain my life back. Sitting in the house for weeks was not going to be good for my family, nor, myself.

I walked into the office, which I worked in for several years now. The Doctors whom I worked for were supportive of my situation, as well as the staff. I was apprehensive upon my return to work. The first day back to work I was welcomed by the whole staff at the front desk. I was a little overwhelmed with the pleasantries. As I preceded downstairs to my desk, I looked at the picture of Matt and I after our triumphant victory with chemotherapy. Our faces were beaming with joy. Of course, I started to cry. God, how am I going to get through each day? As the weeks progressed at the office, the questions of "How are you? This question started to dissipate in everyone's minds. I tried to decipher whether the question was a rhetorical or have truth. How are you doing, as Jackie as a person? How are you doing as the mother whom lost her son?

Dave went back to work the next day, which was grueling for him. Working on the course, where his son gratefully respected. Matt worshiped his father and wanted to know everything how to run a golf course. His career aspirations were set at eight years old. Approaching the first hole the day after the funeral was a surreal experience for Dave.

The Everyday tasks became challenging as the months carried on...

The first day I went to the grocery store, which seems like a simple task for most, became a painful one for me. My life seemed to have a numbing overtone when a simple task had to be accomplished. I walked down the cereal aisle, and my eyes glanced at the "fruity pebbles." That triggered a flashback when Matt threw up his breakfast the morning of the brain tumor diagnosis. I grew more dazed and confused throughout the store. I did not remember what I needed. As I eventually entered the checkout line, I saw a package of the Reese big cup candy. Matt's favorite candy bar. The woman at the checkout said, "Can I help you come through the line?" This was the first time, as I describe a tsunami. An overabundance of Grief and sadness that overtakes my entire body. I start trembling, coughing, and crying which leads to the inability to catch my breath. I looked at the woman and tried to speak, "I can't do this today!" I walked out of the store with a cart of groceries left behind. I sat in my car for several minutes before I drove. As I walked into the kitchen, Dave said, "I thought you were going to the store today?"

I said, "I could not do it today." I went upstairs to our bedroom and slept for over two hours. Dave came upstairs to check if I was okay. "Jackie, are you okay?" I responded, "I will never be the same again." I felt weak when I got up. The rest of the day brought anxiety of what would trigger at bedtime; Flashbacks, tremors, and night sweats.

There must be a better way to deal with my grief:

Throughout my life, I found exercise was my only resource to escape many episodes of traumatic experiences.

At fifteen years old I rode my bike to Elaine Powers to workout. I was by far the youngest person attending classes. My mother had to sign consent so I could participate in the aerobics classes.

While Matt was going through chemotherapy, I walked over to Franklin Field and talked to the security guard there. I said, "My son is going to be in CHOP for at least six months could I come on to the field and walk. I have to get out of the hospital for a while." He said, "Oh, sure. I'll tell all the security guards that you will be coming." I will be forever grateful to the security guards at the University of Pennsylvania. One afternoon, the guard left some tickets for us to go to a Penn football game. Andrew and Dave went to the game.

One of the janitors brought an exercise bike into Matt's room while he was in one of the rounds of chemo. Matt said, "Yeah, I know my mom's crazy. She's working out on my bike and it's supposed to be my bike for physical therapy and my mom is using the bike." The Oncology team thought that was great. One of the Oncologists agreed to my regimen, "Well, we wish that you could get couple other mothers doing some sort of exercise. Some haven't taken a shower in days. They haven't left the hospital."

I'd run on Franklin Field, during the fall months. The stadium was closed during the winter. I needed plan B. What am I going to do now? I would walk from CHOP all the way down to Drexel University, about four miles or so.

Through yoga and deep meditation, my yoga mat was a place to practice relaxation.

On my yoga matt I felt the art of "mindfulness."

After many classes of hot yoga, I found my peace and serenity. The hot yoga released many toxins, which built up over time. The room was over 102 degrees and the sensation of sweating was empowering. I started to sleep better and function on a daily basis. I am a firm believer that exercise transforms the mental clarity through the release of endorphins.

Watching Andrew and Tommy struggle each day without their brother was difficult to observe. Tommy started high school one month after Matt's passing. I knew his journey through Central Bucks East would not be a memorable one without Matt. I was nervous for him every day he walked out the door. Andrew on the other hand, was busy playing baseball and hanging out with friends. The distractions were helpful for Andrew. The grief volcano was about to erupt at some point with both boys.

Tommy's milestones were overshadowed from the loss of his twin....

When it was time for Tommy to go to the prom, it wasn't in the cards. I don't think I could have handled him going to the prom. I dreamt of having a big party for all the kids coming over for grand celebration, as we always have done in the past. My selfish feelings I suppose took the best of me. We didn't have a graduation party for Tommy. He was okay with it. Everything throughout his high school journey was a bittersweet, as well as for myself.

The day before Matt passed, CHOP was on board with the steps for the grieving process. The bereavement team came to the room that morning. "We're going to come to your house in two weeks to check on the boys." Sure enough, I got a call from Jennifer. She came to the house and sat with the boys. We were all dazed and confused from the visit. She spoke in length with Tommy. Jennifer connected more with Andrew because she would play games with him. Younger children respond to adaptive play. After seeing the boys for several weeks, she said, "Tommy needs to see a psychologist; I have a referral from CHOP that would be a great fit for Tommy." Andrew connected by playing the games, and talked about Matt while he was playing Jenga. Tommy needed more assistance. Andrew wasn't at that point of seeking professional therapy.

MAKING A DIFFERNCE THROUGH HOPE

November of 2010, The Brain Tumor Foundation had their annual Race for Hope. The race was held at the Philadelphia Art Museum. From word of mouth, and Matt's memory still fresh in everyone's minds. We managed to gather over 100 people on our **Race for Hope team.** Everyone wanted to give back. The support was overwhelming! We won an award for team spirit. The Cache to this event was the Tee shirt. Everyone on the team purchased a tee shirt. A friend of mine was telling me about creating a THINK GREY tee shirt that everyone could wear on race day. We had a local printing company print the tee shirts. The Grey cancer ribbon symbolized brain cancer awareness. THINK GREY displayed in bold letters, and support brain cancer awareness was just underneath. The entrance fee to the event went to The Brain Tumor Foundation. After the Race for Hope, The Matthew Renk Foundation was in the early stages of becoming a 501C 3 non-profit organizations!

As will many creative minds shall follow, the reward must start out as a dream....

Many sleepless nights in the hospital, as I would lie there staring at the ceiling, I thought to myself, "How can we give back to the hospital? "How can we make a difference in these children's lives and their families?

We started this organization by selling T-shirts and sweatshirts in my basement by word of mouth. After the passing of Matt, The Matthew Renk Foundation was born on September 12, 2011. With an Extraordinary group of passionate people, we were able in just one year, get the official documentation The Matthew Renk Foundation had been declared a 501C3 Organization.

With further research and much planning with our newly appointed board members, we decided in order to make awareness of this insidious disease we needed to start somewhere.

As the months moved on, we decided to start in the school district a Think Grey Day. We went to all the schools that Matt attended, elementary school, middle school and high school to make this awareness. May is brain cancer awareness month. So, in May we were going to make a Think Grey Day. A monumental day for Dave and I, we got the letter from the IRS making us an official nonprofit organization. Dave and I did a chest bump and a high five outside, while we were opening the official documents! The T-shirt sales were amazing; we sold about 500 T-shirts for this historic day. Dave managed to have Phillies Phanatic mascot at the event, to get the students attention. Bridge Valley was Matt's elementary school. Channel 10 news was there to broadcast the day's events. Everywhere I turned I saw the Think Grey T-shirt. Then from Bridge Valley, we went to Holicong Middle School, which was Matt's last school that he attended in the ninth grade. There was a student in the school at that time that was still going through brain cancer. So, that electrified the event even more. The school went a step further, the students made a human cancer ribbon. The advisors went on the roof of the school and took a picture of the cancer ribbon; 1,600 students formed this honorable token in support to the cause.

Andrew at the time was attending Buckingham elementary School. Matt attended K-3 grade there as well. Andrew was proud to see all the support for his brother at his school. We had a busy day going to those schools, but the support was just incredible. Every teacher and guidance counselor had a Think Grey T-shirt on. The final school was Central Bucks East where Tommy was attending. A lot of people didn't know who Matt was because he passed before he got to attend the school. We walked into the auditorium there must have been seventy-five students on stage to show their support. Channel 10 news was interviewing Tommy and the principal upon our arrival.

That evening we all gather around the TV to watch Channel 10 news. The broadcaster said, "The Renk family is starting this new foundation called Think Grey. If you ever heard of Think Pink, now Think Grey to support pediatric brain cancer awareness, in honor of their late son Matthew."

We needed to have a mission statement for our foundation. Our primary mission is to provide much needed emotional and financial support to individuals, and their families facing the challenges associated with pediatric brain cancer. Through the work of The Matthew Renk Foundation, we will continue to fight the challenges presented by this disease and support those most impacted.

As we all sat down at our first board meeting, we all were brainstorming with ideas to raise money for our organization. The small amount of money raised through the T-shirt sales was a great start, but not enough to keep the foundation a float. The first year, we raised over 2,100.00 in T-shirt sales. One of the board members brought to our attention that Lookaway Golf Club wanted to host a memorial golf tournament in honor of Matt.

The whole summer we were preparing for the first Matthew Renk Memorial golf tournament. The Foundation was pulling me in many directions. At that time, I was still working full-time at the surgeon's office. One day I walked into work and I sat at my desk, and felt the Foundation was hanging on my shoulders. There's so much going on. The 501c3 was confirmed. I got Think Grey T-shirts to sell, design a website and organize our first golf tournament.

As I sat confused...

Matt appeared in spirit, he said, "Mom, you got to leave your job. The foundation needs your fire to make this work." That night I had a conversation with Dave. I explained to him of Matt's presence was with me that day at the office. I said, "I got to get this foundation off the ground." Dave said, "Of course, we will work out the logistics." I was trying to explain Matt's spirit was powerful that day. I don't know if Matt's spirit came to him yet. When Matt said, "Mom, you've got to get the hell out of here and get the foundation off the ground." So, I went into work that following Monday and I told the doctors I was resigning from my position at the office.

The hot air balloon needed to take off, the only fire that would ignite this balloon was I...

September of 2011 was the first Matthew Renk Memorial Golf Tournament held at Lookaway Golf Club. This private event was opened for Lookaway members and their guests. The tournament sold out in two days with 110 golfers. The first year we raised over $42,000.00 for the foundation. WOW, this day was truly amazing.

This first year was an impressionable start to such a great cause.

The only cure for my grief was action...

Matt loved golf and what better way to honor his passion, through a memorial golf scholarship at Central Bucks East. The Foundation became a full-time job, and I appointed myself as the foundation director. No matter what type of people that you would have on your board, nobody was going to have a passion as mine. I approached the coach at Central Bucks East and we discussed the criteria for such an award. Matt never got the opportunity to try out for the golf team. He passed before he started high school and his attitude was, I'm not a great golfer, but sure as hell I'm going to try. The scholarship held a certain criteria from the applicant: respect, integrity, sportsmanship and appreciation for the golf course. This was not a merit scholarship. We looked at the applicants' essays and we interviewed each student. Through the interviewing process, we got to know the student.

The scholarship was not a large sum of money, $500 was the amount we rewarded the student. We got to speak to each candidate and get to know their personality. We were not looking for a scratch golfer or a low handicap, or an honor student. We were loking for a student whom exemplified the type of character wthich Matt possessed.

The First Matthew Renk Memorial Golf scholarship for 2012 went to a female student. She amplified all of the characteristics that Matt possesses. She was honored to receive such an award, especially the first recipient.

I was working diligently day in and day out in my little office. The sweat was dripping off my brow. The term working your ass off and sweating while do it was I. Sweating upstairs in our 275-year-old house with the fan blowing me.

Perseverance has always been my best character trait came to fruition...

We applied for the Registered trademark of "THINK GREY" this was a huge undertaken on the part of the patent attorney. Eight months to a year to finally get that trademark. Think Grey was a registered trademark in the eyes of the United States.

Within eighteen months, we had a successful organization: A golf tournament, "Think GREY" day in the school district, golf scholarship, and registered trademark. We're gaining momentum with this organization.

Nothing great can be created without passion...

A year after Matt passed, after the first golf tournament in 2011. A lot was going through Tommy's mind. We asked Tommy to go to the awards night. He said, "No, I can't go!" At this point he started therapy with Dr. Cassano. He started seeing his therapist for eight months. We were standing in the kitchen; Dave and I were ready to give the award out that evening. We said, "Tommy, why don't you come with us?" This was the first time we saw Tommy freak-out. He said, "How do you two think I can get through this? How could you walk around in school with a Think Grey shirt on with my dead brother's name on the back of the shirt? How do you think I can go through this every single day?" He sat down and cried his eyes out. We thought the awards night would be good for him to see what we're doing and to recognize the accomplishment we have made in Matt's memory. He was angry. He also stated, "Mom, all you talk about is the foundation!"

My awareness of my sons' grief was devastating to my soul...

Junior year 2011 Tommy was completely numb. I remember this night vividly. This was a Thursday night in November. It was a really weird night I had to go to a member's house to give them a pin flag from the golf tournament. Tommy was extremely quiet. For a couple months he was extremely quiet and I don't know what was going through his mind. Dave was ready to go to a board meeting. Tommy was driving at the time, and there were times that I got nervous about him driving. Dave said, "Tommy, just left," I said, "I don't know where he went." Dave said, "I'm going to go out in the truck and I'm going to try to find him." They both got in an argument at the house. They were arguing about something and Tommy blew up. He got really angry and Tommy's anger was pretty pronounced. He broke a Ping Pong table during one of his rages of anger. He broke a lot of things in the house. Dave said to him "Let's go down to the shop and talk," He wanted to get him talk and get his anger out. "Let's go down to my office and we'll rip it apart. I don't care."
   Dave's office is situated near the irrigation pond.
   They both went down to the shop.

Tommy was in the middle of a rage. Dave brought him down to the shop and he freaked out and ripped Dave's whole office apart. Dave said, "I don't care. Just throw things. You got to get it out." Tommy took off, didn't know where he went. Dave came flying in the house and he says, "Tommy took off in his truck and I don't know where he was going." He said, "I'm going to go find him!" I'm standing in the kitchen frozen. Oh my God, oh my God what's happening? Dave finally tracks him down in the truck.

Dave told him to come home. Tommy flew out of his truck and ran off into the woods. Dave came back into the house for a second time. He said, "He went in the woods and I got to go find him," I said, oh my God!! Dave got his flashlight, and ran out of the house so fast, that the door rattled in his departure! Dave saw Tommy standing at the edge of the irrigation pond. He said to his father looking at the pond in a desperate tone, "I don't want to be here anymore, I can't live my life without Matt." Dave came running in the house full of mud, with a look of fear that will never be erased from my mind. Dave said, "I have to take him to Doylestown Hospital. Tommy wants to take his life," I said, "Holy shit. Oh my God!" I was just shaking uncontrollably. "I'll call you when we get there." Dave uttered in a frightned tone.

Hours have past, and my anxiety was through the roof....
    Andrew walked in the kitchen, and I tried to regain my composure.
    "Where are Tommy and Dad?" He said in a perplexed tone. I said, "They just went out for a ride."
    At midnight Dave called to let me know what was happening at the Emergency room. Dave said, "He told the doctor that he has suicidal thoughts. So, we have to take Tommy to a psychiatric hospital." I screamed, "Are you kidding me?" Dave said, "Pack a bag for Tommy and I'll meet you in the parking lot at Doylestown Hospital." I said, "Oh, great. Are you frigging kidding me? I just lost a son a year ago and now this?" I called Dr. Cassano as soon as I got off the phone with Dave. I said, "We got to send Tommy to a hospital because he has suicidal thoughts. What do I do?"
    "Well, I'll call my colleague, and call you right back. I'll have him admitted tonight."
    As I started to pack Tommy's bag, my feelings of guilt started to become surreal...
    Was I too wrapped up with the foundation?

Andrew and I arrived at the parking lot of Doylestown hospital.
    I walked over to the truck; Tommy was in a catatonic state. He said, "Mom, I'm sorry." I grabbed him so tight, "I'm sorry, that you have to go through this pain!" Dave came to back of the truck and signaled me to come in his direction. Dave was trembling. "I'll talk to you in a few hours when we get admitted to the hospital. I have directions to a psychiatric hospital in West Philadelphia."

I never went to sleep. Of course, Andrew was scared. He asked me, "Where did Tommy go?" I said, "He had to go to the hospital because he wasn't feeling well." I didn't know how to explain what had happened. I didn't know this was coming and I'm trying to keep it all together. Dave calls me at three o'clock in the morning." "They finally found him a room. This place is awful. I don't want to leave him here, but we need to get him treatment." At 4:30am I hear the truck pulling into the driveway. Dave finally came home, "Jackie, it's the worse place I've ever seen in my entire life. Tommy's rooming with a kid that is just OD'd on drugs," I said, "This is not fair. It's not fair that my son has to be there!"

The next day Tommy called me. I said, "How you doing, Tom?" He said, "Okay, Mom. This place is really weird though." We had to drop Andrew off at his cousin's house because I didn't want Andrew to see his brother yet. We didn't tell much family because it was too hard to comprehend of what state of mind Tommy's was in at the time. Again, I was going through the emotions of this disastrous event.

Mental illness may be described as an abstract diagnosis, opposing to a concrete diagnosis of cancer...

When we arrived at hospital in Philadelphia, I opened up the car door and just threw up my guts all over the lawn. I said to Dave, "I need to get myself together before we head into this place. Are we really here?" "Unfortunately, we are here and we will get through this together." Dave stated in his compassionate tone.

The smell of mental illness hit me as I entered this facility. We had to sit in the lobby until it was time to see Tommy. I said to the cranky receptionist, "Wait, I have to wait outside until your staff allows me to see my son? My son is not a criminal!" Jackie freak-out was in full force.

As we walked down this creepy hallway, Tommy was sitting all by himself in this dark cold room. I thought to myself, there was no way he is staying in this dungeon. As I looked down at his shoes, his shoelaces were removed.

Tommy was there for five grueling days.

Andrew wanted to see his brother! Andrew looked scared as we walked into the hospital. This was a level were a twelve-year-old could not grasp. His brother was practically locked up. Andrew said in the most innocent tone, "How come Tommy doesn't have shoelaces on his shoes?" The voice of Matt entered my mind, "Mom, are you going to yell at the doctors today?" These doctors are starting to piss me off! I'm going to freak on these doctors. We sat with psychologist after our visit with Tommy, I said, "What's this bullshit with the shoelaces removed?" He said, "It's protocol from the hospital that we're not allowed to have shoe-laces or anything that you son could harm himself." I said, "My son had suicidal thoughts." He was in a very catatonic state that night with Dave, a very bad state, but still I know that was protocol of the hospital.

My strength needed to come within myself, not from an outside source...

In the meantime, I fought hard to get Tommy a psychiatrist, who could get him on the right medication, and a pathway from his grief. With a phe-nomenal referral from Dr. Cassano, we found a psychiatrist from CHOP, whom practiced in New Jersey. I did not care how much we had to travel; we needed to support Tommy on this journey.

Tommy was given one medication that night of the incident, but there seemed to be no treatment plan allocated for my son.

Thanksgiving was approaching in a few days...

I said to the attending psychiatrist, "Oh, my son's not staying here Thanksgiving. You're going to go sign the discharge papers and we're get-ting him out of here right now!" I said to myself, is this déjà vu?" I WILL NEVER STOP FIGHTING FOR MY SONS NO MATTER WHAT!

Tommy wasn't eating, nor was he showering. These were all physical signs of deep depression.... His clinical diagnosis was situational depres-sion.

He was in the hospital for five days. We got him out of the hospital two days before Thanksgiving. I knew I needed to make the holiday somewhat festive for my boys. I felt a distraction with family would be helpful. As usual I was trying to make everything great. My mother-in-law just had one of her many surgeries. My son was discharged from psychiatric hos-pital. I made the full Thanksgiving dinner and brought it to my In-laws house.

Perseverance and patience were an uphill climb with this heavy backpack on...

I had nothing left in me after this one. I was working on borrowed time. Another bomb just went off in our house. The grief volcano just started to erupt in all of us.

The most ironic event about thanksgiving night was when my father-in-law put some music on before we all sat down. Of all the songs, to be played at this time was perfect. "Here Without You." The song we played at Matt's funeral. I said, "Everybody stop what they're doing, stop eating, Matt just walked into the room." The family didn't understand what I meant. The spirit of Matt was evident. Matt's here and was sitting right next to Tommy. Why that song came on? I'm not here for Thanksgiving, but I'm here.

Matt comes to us at the most important times....

My whole life seemed to be at a standstill when Tommy came home from the hospital. Taking care of Tommy's emotional state was my #1 priority. We went to go see psychiatrist in Cherry Hill once a week until Tommy was more stable. The psychiatrist was trying to regulate the appropriate medication for his depression.

The loss of his twin was more compounded than any loss, one could ever imagine. I was still trying to keep up with him showering and eating. He dropped a good twenty pounds. All he did was sleep.

Junior year he basically slept. He'd come home from school and sleep. He would see friends here and there, but he found a bunch of friends that he thought were friends. They weren't there for him. He missed the friends that he had with Matt. His friends were having fun and Tommy was going through hell. Tommy took a lot of anger out on Andrew, too. They'd get in some bad fights.

Everything triggered Tommy off. Chairs would be flying constantly. He broke a lot of stuff, but his grief was so compound ... the anger was beyond anybody's anger. The depression was beyond anybody's ... guilt, fear, anxiety, and the loss. There's so much I felt with him. Dr. Cassano said to me after one therapy session, "Mrs. Renk, you lost your son, but Tom lost his twin brother. Tom lost a big part of his life, "losing his right arm and walking around without it for the rest of his life."

We alternate saw Dr. Cassano one week and the next week, the psychiatrist. Both Docs knew each other well which helped with Tommy's treatment planning.

After two years with the Psychiatrist, Tommy was completely off of his medication for depression. After many years with therapy Dr. Cassano, he still checks in periodically.

The years of struggle happened to be the times, which I learned the most about myself...

Physical illness vs. mental Illness

I had the two extremes. The physical part of cancer is this: The physical characteristics are different: hair loss (bald), extreme weight loss, and loss of appetite. The end is just a matter of time. We live in a society that we need take a drug for everything. Physically to make the symptoms dissipate. The other side of the spectrum is Mental illness, the pain nobody wants to talk about. From my experience, emotional pain can be viewed as abstract. The physical symptoms are not visible. Individuals' experience these types of pain tend to bury the emotions. After Tommy had his breakdown, no one asked, "how is Tommy doing? The focus was on Matt 's cancer diagnosis. Please stop looking at the physical aspect of illness because Matt lost his hair. Tommy lost his mind!

After Matt's hair was growing back and putting on weight ... the comments were observed as visible signs of healing. Oh, Matt looks good. We were held as prisoners to cancer. It doesn't go away. Just because I got dressed and blew out my hair today doesn't mean I'm doing well. I put on a good show on for many years. The performance is over.... The tap shoes have worn out.

I've been to hell and back a couple times...

Matt and Tommy's birthday after the loss...

This bittersweet celebration must go on. Tommy's turning sixteen and he's going to be driving. This birthday was a big milestone. How do we celebrate your first birthday without his twin brother?

Tommy liked the chocolate chip cake and Matt liked ice cream cake. Picking up the candles #1 and #6 at the grocery store, made me pause in the aisle

Someone give me the strength to get through this day. I was trying to put my mind in overdrive. I've got to move on for Tommy. I had to put a lid on my own emotions. We decided to have family and some friends to support Tommy! We always had the twins' birthday parties were huge, fifty to seventy people. Both boys had different friends and their twin friends.

I had this idea that we would celebrate Tommy's birthday, but we couldn't forget Matt. I decided I was going to do a balloon release in honor of Matt for his birthday. Everybody came over for the celebration. I gave each person balloon to whoever was there, the seventeen-balloon had a big smile face on it and I gave it to Tommy. The ironic piece to this day, when we all released the balloons, Tommy hesitated for a few moments, then released his oversized balloon. The balloon actually got stuck in the tree, came back down, the smile face turned around and looked at Tommy. The balloon stayed in the tree for months. This event is just another example of Matt's spirit coming back us in a different ways. I'm still here. No matter what I am still here.

Making the connection with CHOP....

Great things are not done by impulse, but little increments at a time...

I have something to present to the hospital now. We have the foundation registered as a non-profit 501c3, THINK GREY trademark, scholarship, an annual golf tournament to raise funds for the foundation, and Think Grey Day to raise awareness for pediatric brain cancer. How am I going to make the connection? How can this foundation be intertwined with the largest children's hospital in the country?

I'm about to climb Kilimanjaro.

I spoke with one of the Social workers in neuro-oncology. "You got to get connected with the partnership at the hospital." She described so supportively. I connected with the senior director of partnership. In our conversation, I expressed how the foundation wanted to make awareness at the hospital.

His notion to my proposal was as follows:

"The hospital has many foundations that support the hospital." I said, "I don't think there's too many foundations that are geared towards direct donation to families."

"Well, let me go with your intensions, to the powers to be, and formulate how we can work with THE MATTHEW RENK FOUNDATION. I was still conversing back and forth with CHOP.

Maybe, just maybe my dream, which was created by many sleepless nights with Matt, will become a reality! Alex was one of the first pediatric brain cancer patients at the hospital and if you've seen Alex's Lemonade Stand, she actually started her organization as a lemonade stand outside her home raising money for pediatric brain cancer

It took me six months to organize the next Think Grey Day at the hospital. I asked the director, "Well, we're on the topic of Think Grey Day. Can we put the CHOP logo on the T-shirt? How can we do that?"

"Wow. You got a lot of energy," the director stated in excitement. We made a donation to the hospital with the revenue from the golf tournament. The Matthew Renk Foundation donated funds to Oncology Relief Fund. This fund is to support funds to families while their children are receiving treatment at the hospital. For example, parking, gas, lodging, and food.

While you child is in treatment a parent needs to stay with the child. The caretaker may be with the patient for days, weeks, months, and years. These long inpatients hospital stays cause for expenses to accumulate. The utility bills are still coming to the house.

These families are under a tremendous amount of stress.

May 6, 2012 was a sea of kids, and this was the day that I was going to honor my son, and other students who passed away from brain cancer. The adrenaline was pumping inside me! I knew my speech about my Matt was ahead of me, and Andrew was in the audience. Andrew was a student of Holicong at the time. My composure needed to be laser focused. No time to loss it in front of his classmates. I was patiently waiting in hallway of the school, and turned to see the commotion in a distance, to find that the Phanatic and Swoop just arrived. These mascots represent the Philadelphia sports teams. I broke out into a sweat. Just moments away from rallying up these students with the mascots trailing behind. I had my Think Grey shirt on, my cap on looking like a teenager. I wanted to meld with all the other kids. Trying to make the awareness of pediatric brain cancer. Especially when this disease had stricken two of their fellow classmates in less than two years. Our mission was to remember and never forget our friends.

The students performed the human cancer ribbon for the second year, waiting for the event to begin. The nerves were starting to raddle me as I moved further onto the blacktop. You could hear a pin drop when I walk out. I said, "We're here today to honor, remember and never forget. We lost two of your fellow classmates in two years to pediatric brain cancer, and we're here today to remember these students. I lost my son to two years ago and we're here to celebrate all they have given to us as friends, and as a community." I spoke about our foundation and how we support families through emotional and financial support. I had to change gears real fast to get theses mascots out to the crowd. I said," it's my honor to present to you today the biggest mascots in Philadelphia!" The music started playing and the mascots came flying out with the Think Grey T-shirts. They were dancing with the kids. Everyone was glad to be a part of this Memorable Day.

Conquering my fears has been my secret to my success...

The second golf tournament was a torrential downpour. I mean, it rained so hard, but it didn't stop the golfers. The determined golfers still played fourteen holes in the pouring rain. This was the type of rain that you shouldn't be outside, but these golfers were determined to play with their rain suits on. I said, "Wow, these golfers really are here for the cause."

In year two of the golf tournament, we raised $75,000. Again; the event was sold out in three days, with golfers on a waiting list.

Now, the foundation was taking off with generous support from the membership at Lookaway Golf Club. We can now start the direct donations to families. I connected with neuro-oncology and radiation oncology to expedite this process. We wanted the funds from the foundation to go directly to the families. These families could be inpatient or out - patient. We started an application for financial assistance, which the social workers would have the families fill out to apply for funds from the Foundation. As of today, the foundation has directly donated to 350 patients and their families. As soon as I got notification, via email from the social workers, I made sure I got a check in the mail ASAP. Our foundation has kept electricity on, paid mortgages, beds for children to sleep in, food, lodging, Airfare to the US for treatment, and funerals. For many years at Christmas time, we had a TOYS FOR CHOP drive, which we accumulated many gifts for children and their siblings to make their holiday a little brighter.

Respite Garden: Healing through green space...

The latter part of the third year the Foundation was inducted into the Founder Society of CHOP. For an organization to be a part of this group, a considerable donation to the hospital needs to be meet. Some organizations have donated thousands to millions of dollars to be a member of the Founders Society.

I got an unbelievable call from the senior director of the partnership. He said, "Jackie, I have an idea for you that you've been waiting for a long time." I said, "Oh my God. Let me sit down. This is big." He stressed in his tone." CHOP is building an outpatient ambulatory center called the Berger Center.

The center will be the state-of-the art facility. I've got a great idea for your foundation. On the sixth floor will be rooftop respite garden. The hospital was thinking if the Matthew Renk Foundation could be a part of this roof top project? It's a pretty substantial piece of property, approximately 1400 square feet and costs a substantial amount of money. This would be a place where patients and families can go while undergoing treatment. There will be a running track where the kids can go for physical therapy. You were the first person I thought of because I know what you've been through, and your dream was to build something at the hospital for families. I'm going to connect you to a representative that's a part of the philanthropic part of the hospital."

I got off the phone, and thought to myself, *this is exactly what the foundation needs to be a part of.* I want to do something huge for the hospital; I brought this idea to Dave's attention. He said, "this idea sounded really good, but are we going to be able to afford this? "I said, "Oh, we can have a few more golf tournaments, with the rate in which the foundation is headed we can do this!"

The rooftop garden would overlook the entire skyline of Philadelphia. So, there were two other elements to the garden that were needed to purchase. The benches to sit in the garden came with a price tag as well.

One bench didn't have a back to it and the other one had a back to it. We presented the notion to Andrew and Tommy. Both boys agreed to the idea. Tommy was funny; he stated, "Well, I don't want to get the bench that doesn't have the back to it because I don't want anybody sitting on my name." He had a point there. We purchased the one that has a backing to it and then we left the other bench if somebody wanted to buy the bench. I wanted the whole garden and the benches in there, but I thought maybe it would have been repetitious of buying two benches. So, Andrew and Tommy bought the other bench in memory of their brother. 'In Memory of Matthew Renk, Andrew and Tommy Renk.' The signage for the entrance to the garden stated this garden was provided by: *The Matthew Renk Foundation.* The Founder's Society were flabbergasted that we bought a portion of this respite garden.

In May, the Founder Society held the event at Merion Golf Club. Merion Golf Club is one of the top ten golf courses in the world, located in Ardmore, Pennsylvania.

In 2009, Matt volunteered for the Walker Cup during his remission phase. He was a volunteer for the grounds crew. When he left that day, he said the golf course superintendent, "Matt, I'll see you in 2013 at the US Open because I'm going to volunteer. I'll be eighteen years old; I will be driving my truck down here without my dad, I'll see you then!" Unfortunately, Matt passed in 2010 and he didn't have that opportunity.

In 2014 we made our first endowment to the respite garden. At the Founder Society event, A family told their story how CHOP supported their child through their journey. When the foundation got the invitation that year. I said, "I'm going to that event and I'm going to tell Matt's story. I phoned the chairperson of the event and asked, "Do you have a speaker for this year?" she said, "No. We're are working to get a family." I said, "I got to tell my story that night. Is CHOP ready to hear my story? I've been there for all the triumphant stories. They're good stories of how the hospital has helped the kids through heart surgery, and all the successful journeys. My story ended tragically."

She said, "I know your story, but I know what you've done, everyone needs to hear your story. Let me make a few phone calls and I'll call you back." Within an hour and a half, she calls me back, "You're in. You're going to speak at the Founder Society. I digressed for a few minutes to myself. "I'm speaking at Merion where Matt wanted to be at the 2013 U.S Open. This is the arena where I need to be to tell the story. She calls me back two days later and said, "I know you're speaking at the Founder Society, but would you like to speak to the staff at the hospital?" I said, "Sure." "Well, it's in two weeks," I said, "Okay. I will do my best."

Dave drove me down to the hospital. I was escorted into a large conference room, and then greeted by many staff members from CHOP. This speech was my practice round, I presumed. I prepared a PowerPoint that prompted me to tell Matt's story. It was so empowering for me, as well as the staff. The whole staff gave me a standing ovation. Every staff member approached me and complimented on my powerful story. "You blew the socks off of all these people here and this is a great preparation for Merion." Thank God I got a few weeks to be fully prepared for the next event. A writer and an editor wanted to edit my speech. I said, "I'm sorry, sirs, but this can't be edited. It comes from my heart, it's tough to tell but only can be told by me. You want it from my toes?" "Exactly", the both gentlemen agreed. I said, "Okay. I'll deliver." We had a conference call discussing the pictures that would be in the presentation. In reflection form the last presentation, I felt that I was not organized, somewhat jumbled in my delivery. It was the first time I told my story. The team wanted to write my speech. I said, "I can't write it. You don't know the story." The team was adamant regarding the context of the speech.

Life is not measured of how many breaths we take, it's the moments that take your breath away....

In life you may get that one time to shine. This was that night.

As the four of us were in the car driving up 76 on the Schuylkill Expressway heading towards the golf course, the rain was coming down in buckets. I couldn't even speak in the car because I was so nervous. Dave and the boys were talking incessantly.

My in-laws were going to meet us at the event. A few foundation members were coming for support as well. I wanted my father and siblings to attend, but all opted out that night. Dave said, "No one understands how important this night is to you." This was living the legacy of my son. As we pulled up to the golf course, the tears started rolling down my face. The emotions of what could have been started to unfold.

I got out of the car, and the sun was shining over the horizon on hole #13. I felt so empowered at this time the adrenaline was pumping now, because guess who's here? Matt's Spirit was there off the horizon.

The vision was gorgeous as the sun radiated over this course, which was built in 1912. A top-ten golf course where Matt wanted to be, and his mom was there speaking on his behalf. As I walked in to this majestic clubhouse, many people from CHOP greeted me. Why does everybody know who I am? Oh, you're the keynote speaker? Pictures were flashing. People telling us where we have to be and do I have enough water. Did you eat? You're really making me nervous. As the nerves started to comply in my mind. The crowd started to multiply throughout the room.

Everybody suggested for me to eat something. I said, "No, because I'll probably throw up. Water would be sufficient." I went to the bathroom a couple times, due to the butterflies fluttering in my stomach. An older gentleman came over and tapped me on the shoulder, in a whisper tone, "fifteen minutes to show time." Oh my God, I said to myself. We're talking the CEO and CFO of hospital are here! The trustee of the board was highlighting what the Founder Society was all about. Alludes to the keynote speaker for tonight. "Tonight, we have Jackie Renk that started a foundation in honor of her late son."

Then the CEO of the hospital enters the podium. At this point I'm standing next to him and my knees were starting to buckle. This is not the time to lose my composer. The CEO was going to introduce me. He starts talking about our foundation and the impact, which we made on the hospital. Someone behind me taps me on my shoulder and asks me, "You're doing this off the cuff?"

I replied, "Yes."

"How are you going to do this without cards?" I pointed to my heart.

The CEO came up beforehand and asked me, "where are your notecards?" OMG! With the notecards! I don't need notecards. I just had my PowerPoint of my pictures of Matt, Matt and Tommy and Andrew and the Foundation. He states. "Without any more introduction, I present to you this evening, Jackie Renk, the Director and Founder of the Matthew Renk Foundation. It's show time. I get the podium and I felt stiff. I felt like this isn't me. I stepped down from the podium with my microphone. Now, I feel more comfortable. I wanted my composure to be engaging. As I faced the audience, I hesitated until all eyes were on me. I started off my speech. "What do you do when you get the worse news, that no parent ever wants to hear, that your son has a brain tumor?" Nobody moved. The audience was paralyzed. As I gazed over to the CEO and CFO, I noticed the tears in their eyes. The gentlemen were astounded by my journey.

The emotion that was running through me was so overpowering. Matt kept me going. The power of Matt was radiating through me. I was stoic throughout the whole presentation. My theatrical expression showed emotion, but my tears remained calm. I went into detail of my long journey with CHOP and all the aspects that changed me along this journey. I highlighted the respite garden and how this green space, was only a dream and now became a reality. The staff that was employed at CHOP during my journey, and the compassion which each of them showed each day towards these children. The staff kept me going for over two years.

The presentation was held in oldest part of the clubhouse. As I looked over at the bookcase, I noticed the plaques of Bobby Jones, Ben Hogan, and Arnold Palmer. I had chills at this point when I spotted the "LEGENDS OF GOLF." I said," Please, allow me to digress for a minute, tonight we are at a top ten golf course in the world, and my son wanted to be here." I segued into Matt's history about golf and how important it was for him to attend the 2013 U.S Open, which was held at Merion. I'm here in his place. At the end of the speech, the clapping felt that it went on forever. The CEO came back on the microphone. He stated in a profound tone, "That was the most amazing speech I've ever heard in my entire life."

My three sons gave me the courage, integrity, spirit ....

The CEO and the CFO came over to me later that evening. "That's a hell of a story and I never heard anybody tell a story like that. How did you do it without cards?"

Of all the presentations, which I presented over the years, Merion was my greatest speeches ever given...

Success of my accomplishments shines in my heart...

As of 2020, The Matthew Renk Foundation has raised over $900.000 in revenue to support children and their families to combat pediatric brain cancer. With the continued support from the membership of Lookaway Golf Club, this organization continues to generate more than double the amount in the first year in hosting this memorial golf tournament, which is held every fall.

The foundation has directly donated to over 350 families since the start in 2011. Through the work of this organization, we have found healing as a family, as a community, and to live the driven spirit of Matt.

For more information about the Matthew Renk Foundation: Please go to our website: Matthew Renk Foundation.org

Where did our marriage go?

Tommy was ending his senior year of high school, when our marriage was heading towards a downward spiral. Dave and I were just going through the motion of our lives. I felt as though Dave was not dealing with Matt's death for about two years. I, on the other hand, dug into the foundation as my coping mechanism. Dave kept on chugging through work and showed less of his feelings. We got to a point which we just stopped communicating. Through reading many books on grief, I learned that seventy-five percent of marriages fail after a loss of a child. I knew we were heading in that direction. After three years after Matt's passing, I need to find myself and started seeing a therapist on a weekly basis. I tried seeking a bereavement counselor in the beginning, but the tsunamis were too intense.

In the eyes of others, I was acting too selfish....

There are many reasons why couples separate, and the assumptions, which were made to my character, was not acceptable to me. I let everyone have his or her opinion. As I reiterate, "walk in my shoes" and then pass judgment. Dave and I had many short conversations on how do we move forward with our marriage? Dave had a way of compartmentalize the situation. My job was to keep everyone moving on this freight train. We would spend time together as at dinnertime and that was the extent of the connection.

When I told Dave that I decided to move out of the house, he was surprised at first, but he knew I was serious. We were falling out of love because all of our grief was heading towards us.

After six weeks, I found an apartment 15 minutes from the house. I wanted to be close to the boys so the distance would not be a factor to this situation. I knew I had a hurdle bigger than my height to be of a concern. We needed to break the news to the boys.

After the one-year leased was signed, I knew my decision was real. The ironic piece to the decision was that day I approached the apartment steps, a butterfly followed me up the steps to the door. This moment validated my decision of where I needed to be. Two weeks after I signed the lease Tommy graduated from high school. Dave asked me, "When are you moving out of the house?' I was already paying the rent, but not living in the apartment yet. I told him, "I will tell the boys next weekend."

Saturday morning when I woke up, I knew this was my last day at the house. Dave brought Tommy to the kitchen. Dave said, "Mom and I are separating for a while." Tommy immediately put his head down and started to cry." I felt so awful inside to see him upset for something that was not his fault. All children blame themselves for the brake up. Dave reassured Tommy that this separation was nothing that he had done.

After several quiet moments from Tommy, He said," Do you want me to help you move?" I was surprised by his offer. Dave and Tommy went to the apartment later that afternoon to move my belongings. Tommy was stoic throughout the move. I came back to the house after everything was moved in because I did not want to sleep at the apartment until I told Andrew.

Andrew returned from caddying that evening. I told him everything that we stated to Tommy earlier that morning. Of course, he was angry and very upset. I said, "You can come to the apartment and stay as long as you want." He was pretty quiet for a while as well.

My Dad and brother were optimistic about the separation. On the other hand, my sister and I got into many arguments with her regarding my choice to separate. Her support throughout my journey thus far, has been more than appreciative.

After one month of the separation, the boys were not answering my phone calls. Tommy stopped at the apartment once, and looked uncomfortable throughout his visit. Andrew came over twice, and both times cried during his visit. Andrew stated many times, "I can't handle you and Dad apart!" Dave started therapy after the separation.

6 weeks later...

Dave and I meet with a mediator to start the divorce proceedings.

The only conversations we had were about the separation and how could I have done this to our family? I knew his intensions were not deliberate; he was having a tough time. We argued on most phone calls, but we managed to be civil when the boys were around.

As the summer came to a close, Tommy was still not speaking to me. Andrew stayed at the apartment overnight, and the next morning we went to visit my Dad at the shore.

As we started preparation for the golf tournament that fall, I knew Dave and I needed to spend more time together to prepare for the event. I called

Dave and asked him if I could come over to get the awards ready for the tournament. His reply was "Sure, come over this afternoon." I thought to myself, well, this is a good sign maybe he is adjusting better to the separation. I was nervous as I pulled up the driveway. I hope this visit goes well today, I thought to myself. Dave was in the kitchen emptying the grocery bags and making lunches for the boys. I said, "You seem to be adjusting well." He said, "I'm not doing well!"

We finished our work for the golf tournament. Dave said, "Do you want to go to the Pineville Tavern for lunch?" We generally had a great time. This was the first time in 6 months that we spoke civilized without our usual screaming matches.

Tommy was coming home later that afternoon. Dave said, why don't you stay at the house for a while and hang out with the boys? Tommy came right up to me and sat right next to me. He said, "Are you staying for dinner?" I replied, "Do you want me to stay?" He responded, Mom, I want you to come back home!!" Andrews's anger was evident. He ate dinner, and left immediately after he was finished. After dinner was over, while we were cleaning up, Dave said," Even though the boys are confused of your visit, it was great to have you here for dinner. Do you want to take a cart ride after we are through cleaning up?"

The golf course has been the stage for discussion…

Dave and I have taken our evening cart rides for over twenty-three years at Lookaway. So, many discussions were had on this golf course. I've had many discussions with Matt, Tommy and Andrew as well. Our family cart rides brought numerous nostalgic moments to the Renk family. I don't know if it's just the atmosphere that makes one more boisterous or whom one may accompany. The golf course has been a stage for discussion: Business decisions are sealed, friendships are rekindled, and new friendships are made.

A second shot may be the only shot one may need. When you get a bad lie, it's all about the second shot in golf, and that night it was about to be a second shot for Jackie and Dave…

Dave wanted to spend more time with me that night. I said, "Why haven't you called me to see if we could work on our relationship?" He said, I had to leave you alone, "because that what you needed."

I knew at that point we needed to give each other another shot.

We would meet each other on dates as time moved on. I started to feel that a spark might have ignited this flame back in our hearts. I started to miss him more and more as I was alone in my apartment. The boys were thrilled that Mom and Dad were seeing each other on a regular basis.

After eight weeks of dating each other, Dave came to the apartment and told me, "The divorce papers are drawn up. What do you want to do?"

I said, "No, I cannot go through with the divorce. We both needed time to heal our wounds, which accumulated over twenty-two years of marriage. Our lives were put to the test the day Matt and Tommy were born, and we never quite dealt with that painful ordeal. The trauma was never dealt with as the years moved on. We as a couple were always in survival mode.

Along the way we lost some friends. Dave perception was that friends wanted to help us through our issues. I wasn't going to tell anyone our personal issues. Everyone's issues were miniscule compared to our issues.

Happiness only exists with acceptance...

We decided to take a trip to Jamaica. Dave did all the planning for the tropical getaway. We "retie the knot ceremony" in Jamaica at the end of that year.

Five years later...

Andrew was finally dealing with Matt's death.

Dave and I were watching the final round of the Masters. Andrew came back from caddying later that afternoon. He washed his truck and went out for the evening. He said nothing to Dave and I that night.

Later that evening, after several attempts of calls and texts, there was no response from Andrew! He was going through a rebellious stage. I left a message on his voicemail, "You better answer the phone! Then I said something I shouldn't have said, "Well, then don't come home tonight." I tossed and turned all night. I finally gave up trying to sleep. I called Andrew again. He finally answered the phone. I said, "What's going on, Andrew?" He responded in a defensive tone, "I'm getting ready to go to school." I said, "No, you're not going to school yet. Come home. We need to talk." He walked in the house extremely distraught and very sad. "I need help, Mom." I said, "Oh my God, sit down. You'll go to school later. We need to deal with this right now. Sit down and let me make you breakfast." So, we sat and we talked for hours.... "Mom, I'm so confused. I don't know what's going on. My friends don't understand, I have no one to talk to, and I feel alone. I said, "I think everything is compounding on you, Andrew. You haven't dealt with Matt's death. You were too young to understand." He started crying. I said, "You don't need to carry those cinderblocks of grief that I told you about forever. You need to release those cinderblocks and put them down. You don't need to carry that weight with you all the time."

I told Tommy that Andrew was having a tough time with dealing with Matt's death. I needed him as his other brother, to help him get through this journey of therapy. Tommy said, I'll take Andrew to Dr. Cassano for you." Dave called Dr. Cassano, to let him know that Andrew needed to start therapy. Tommy drove Andrew to therapy the very next day. I said, "How did Dr. Cassano go today?" Andrew replied, "Well, Tommy hogged up all the time. I needed to talk to him." Dr. Cassano did say that Andrew was depressed, and would need to come for a while. Of course, if Andrew felt that he needed to talk. Andrew was confused how therapy worked. When I drove him one day to therapy, he freaked out in the car while I was driving. He said, "Why does our family have to go through this? I don't remember how this happened to my brother, and this is so unfair!" He punched the passenger window. The anger was radiating through my car now. I said, Andrew, just let it out!"

Andrews's grades were slipping at school. That was not as important compared to the emotional trauma that was settling in Andrew's mind.

No sibling should ever endure such pain…

My boys were swimming in a pool of grief, and I can't rescue them.

Andrew was 11 years old when Matty passed and dealing with many issues of grief, adolescence, school, friends and making great choices. I knew eventually he would get to this point, but didn't know when he was going to deal with the death of his brother. Now, five years later, he was finally dealing with his brother's death. He was going through all those grief phases. As a mother, it gave me great pain to watch the domino effect that our family endured. My energy was a flat tire. Tommy's therapy journey gave support to Andrew's experience to expression his emotions. Andrew was just way too young to even wrap his head around the loss.

The Pain never goes away, we get used to the void that can never be replaced.

No Days off for Andrew...

After many rounds of caddying, hard work pays off.

Andrew opened up a checking account after all his earnings from Caddying that year. Andrew was determined to buy his first truck at sixteen years old. After careful observation with Dave, Andrew found a truck for purchase. As Andrew sat at the car dealer, he opened up his checkbook and wrote his first check! As proud parents, we carefully watched this hardworking young man write a check with pride. I thought the salesman was going to fall off his chair. He said, "A sixteen-year-old is buying his own truck with cash, this is quite remarkable."

The spirit of Matt filters through all four of us in some sort of way.

Andrew at sixteen was trying to find himself, trying figure out where he needs to be. Coping with the catastrophe of losing his brother, his parents separated for a year, almost on the verge of getting divorced. The entire trauma of what has happened to this boy never goes away. Over time, everyone has forgotten our loss. Both boys were trying to put these pieces back together in their lives. That puzzle piece was lost. The piece will always be missing, and that's where we still struggle each day. There are only four plate settings at our table. The empty seat will retain in our hearts. I try so hard keeping all four of us together. I'm hell-bent about our family Sunday dinner.

Matt had a potential work ethic was only a dream to him. At thirteen years old, just before his diagnosis, he wanted those employment working papers. He went down to the office, and fought a great argument. "I want my working papers because I am working for my dad!" Right before Matt got sick, he made a timecard for himself. Dave couldn't pay him, but he would clock in and out just like the other guys. He just wanted to work. All he wanted to do was to work on that golf course! He would spend time with his friends.

He had this all planned out that he was working all summer and he was going to buy himself a truck, a Dually truck.

When we moved to Lookaway and all the boys knew was watching the construction of the golf course. At two years old the boys watched the golf course come alive before their eyes. When we were back in the Cherry Hill house on the bitter cold days, I'd put their snowsuits on and we'd take a walk. I've always had my kids outside. I never was the type of person to be indoors, so was that their personality or was that what I engrained in them or was the atmosphere we brought to our sons? His dreams were to be a golf course superintendent and when Matt was in remission, he sat next to the President of the golf course and said, "Mr. Waldman, I'm going to take my dad's job when he retires!" Mr. Waldman said, "Matt, I really hope I'm still here."

Where does a mother's heart go to fill the emptiness in grey times before and after?

The heart will never the same. I have a hole in your heart that cannot be repaired, even by hands of a cardiac surgeon. At first your heart bleeds and never stops. The hole in your heart that carries you wherever you go. As life moves on one day at a time. If you laugh you feel guilty. If you cry, you never stop crying. It takes one event or situation that triggers the pain. When I would see another mom going through milestones with their children my reflection would be mostly, that could have been us too. I guess others may take those cherished moments for granted. The quiet times reflect the triumph of my accomplishments. The grey times often reflect on the question why? Some times in the grey days of reflection, I think to myself I lived the worst nightmare any mother could not even phantom. These times lead me to isolation.

Isolation was my way of coping. Avoidance was another tool as well. I would loathe the annoying question, day after day; I don't know how you do it? I wanted to avoid the awkward silence after the question was answered. No one knew what to say, or how to comfort me. Perhaps, no one would want to put themselves in these shoes, those painful shoes that I walk in every day.

After tragedy can we ever be the same? No, it changes us forever.

How are you doing as Jackie, or how are you doing with the loss of your son? So, I tried to decipher what that question meant, so I would start asking people when they would ask me, I would answer, "How am I doing as a person, Jackie, or how am I coping with the loss of my son?" There were no words for me at the time. That was a petrifying rhetorical question that was asked frequently.

This was a journey, a compelling journey to move on…

To walk in my son's room weeks after he had past, brought the excruciating pain back again. Nothing was touched or displaced for over three months since his last night he slept in his bed. His suitcase was still packed from CHOP, and has never been unpacked. I did not want to touch that suitcase. I wasn't ready to unpack it, and I knew if I did go into his room, I would start looking through his pictures. I felt as though I had to keep going through this painful journey looking at his pictures and trying to carry on. Eventually, I kept his door closed for several months.

Andrew and Tommy slept on the 3rd floor part of the house. After chemo, Matt painted a room on the second floor and made it his own. The vision of him painted his room with that beautiful baldhead brings a smile to my face.

A monarch butterfly comes through in spirit....

Reflection on my faith and Religion

Why would God Take my son away from me?

Catholicism was the chosen faith instituted for many generations in my family. As a Catholic, I was actively in adherence to all forms of doctrinarian to the Christian faith. Those religious beliefs are different for me today. Religion is a social-cultural system of beliefs, in which we are told to be of supreme importance.

I believe in the spirit of the afterlife.

The other side is a peaceful place of beauty...

With much research through the philosophy of the afterlife, I have learned of such a place. The detailed description from what I have read and researched on the other side: There is no sickness, nor pain. The landscape is of something, which has been vision. The sun shines all the time!! A place that is truly amazing. Once I read and done my research, my reflection on my faith made more sense to me. My burden of my grief was lifted. Matt loved to be outside, he was free from pain! Matt has been on the other side for ten years now, and he built this amazing golf course for us to play when we meet again someday....

I thoroughly believe that that I'm not afraid of dying. Matt's spirit is alive in all of us. Matt comes when I call on him. It may not be right now, but when I least expect his visit, he'll give me some sort of a sign—either through a song played, a butterfly flying around me on the golf course, or a frog sitting on my front porch. Matt's friend came two weeks after the funeral and planted a tree in his memory. That's Matt coming through in his friend to plant the tree.

We tried to go back to church after Matt passed. We were not getting any comfort or spirituality from the Sunday services. What are we doing?

I made a place of solitude for myself. Going to yoga every Sunday morning was my church. Through deep mediation and reflection, I became a better person, for that I am grateful. Going to yoga at least once a week, and made a conscience point twice a week because that was my solitude. Every Sunday morning, I consider yoga my church. That's where I go. As Jesus Christ said, "You can pray anywhere." Prayer can be spoken anywhere.

Thinking about the scoreboard in the sky. The Catholic Church preys on the congregation to be present on Sunday. I respect everyone's beliefs. As the saying states, "don't judge me until you walked a mile in my shoes." So, don't judge me. I've lost a lot of friends along the way and I've gained some new friends. Some friends that I thought that were going to be with me throughout this journey, they were there for a while, but they left because I have changed. I changed with the loss of my son. I've changed with the maturity of being in my 50s and my episodes of trauma that changed my life. Where did she go? You're supposed to bury your son and move on with your life?

I'm happy because I look beyond my imperfections and mistakes that I have made along the way.

I was so afraid and even when we go back to the beginning of my life before all this happened, I was always the peacemaker always waiting for the shoe to drop, waiting for an explosion to happen in my house.

Where am I going in my life and what is important in life! I know I'm making an impact on those children at CHOP.

I was there and I walked in those very uncomfortable shoes. Every time I get an email from the hospital, that a family is in need of financial support. I put my grief aside to support those families; no matter what's happening in my day I make sure I fulfill that grant to that family! As painfully as it may be, to writing out that check with my son's name on the letterhead. When I drop the check in that mailbox, it's Matt dropping in the mailbox. I didn't have the foundation and keep striving for something else that I think I wouldn't be here. I think that the depression would have put me under. It wouldn't give me the strength that I have today.

These shoes are too uncomfortable to walk in, so if you just and I think we as individuals, we walk away from pain. I couldn't walk away from this pain. I had to carry on and I had to keep moving on. There's always that judgment that, oh she's now dealing with what's going on, that's not it, it's the day that I'm having and I think I dealt with my son's death rather remarkable of taking a tragedy and being in a triumph right now and knowing every day I continue to grant my son's wish, of taking care of others. That's exactly what I'm doing, every year the foundation gets bigger. We are helping out more kids. That is what makes me happy and joyful inside that we're able to live my son's legacy.

My accomplishments in my life outweigh my disappointments. I've accomplished so

much in my life as far as having my twins, struggles with developmental delays, another pregnancy, dealing with cancer and my sons' death. The accomplishments helped me pick myself back up.

I overcame many struggles in my life, which I have discovered, more of some profound accomplishments: A profound learning disability, which was not recognized until I was 15 years old. The humiliation of my disability became a struggle in my daily life. I kept on fighting. At fifty-two I went back to school to get my college degree.

Throughout my childhood, I had to grow up really fast in order to survive. I had to make good decisions, take care of myself and care for my brother. My mother was sedated much of my life. Those coping skills were established rapidly at a young age.

I've had to work on being joyful. Even through the suit of armor I wore to hide myself. I've tried to always look for a positive. I have two other children, and both boys got me through a lot of the pain. Dave and I still struggle with the past. I've always taken a little bit of joy and had to run with it because I think if I focused on all the pain I wouldn't be here today.

After twenty-six years of what I have seen and experienced, I f I were given this road to pass through again, I would never take the detour. I have grown to be a physically and an emotionally strong woman. I know who I am, and I have the capacity to accomplish anything…

Tommy has grown to be an extraordinary golf course superintendent, with great aspirations to follow in his father's footsteps, as his twin brother aspired to do.

Andrew has become a determined young entrepreneur and his career path has given him nothing but success!

The joy still holds true the impact that I have made on own children, and lives of children with special needs. Today, I am making a difference every day in children's lives with learning disabilities. Everyday my heart has been overflown with joy of what a difference I have made in a life of a child. Life is about making an impact....

That's a hell of an accomplishment!

CPSIA information can be obtained
at www.ICGtesting.com
Printed in the USA
BVHW040150110821
614170BV00010B/146/J